CHOOSE THE
RIGHT WO

CHOOSE THE RIGHT WORD

An entertaining and easy-to-use
guide to better English –
with **70 test yourself quizzes**

ROBIN HOSIE & VIC MAYHEW

howtobooks

Published by How To Books Ltd
Spring Hill House, Spring Hill Road
Begbroke, Oxford OX5 1RX
United Kingdom
Tel: (01865) 375794
Fax: (01865) 379162
info@howtobooks.co.uk
www.howtobooks.co.uk

First published 2012

How To Books greatly reduce the carbon footprint of their books by sourcing their
typesetting and printing in the UK.

British Library Cataloguing in Publication Data
A catalogue record for this book is available from the British Library

ISBN: 978 1 84528 499 2

Cover design by Baseline Arts Ltd, Oxford
Produced for How To Books by Deer Park Productions, Tavistock, Devon
Designed and typeset by PDQ Typesetting Ltd, Newcastle-under-Lyme, Staffordshire
Printed and bound in Great Britain by Bell & Bain Ltd, Glasgow

NOTE: The material contained in this book is set out in good faith for general
guidance and no liability can be accepted for loss or expense incurred as a result of
relying in particular circumstances on statements made in the book. Laws and
regulations are complex and liable to change, and readers should check the current
position with the relevant authorities before making personal arrangements.

Preface

There may be a smidgeon of truth in the proposition that those who read books on usage don't need them, and those who need them don't heed them. But in the rich broth that is the English language there is always something new and worthy of attention bubbling to the surface. Rules that once seemed inviolable may be challenged and found wanting. A preposition is placed at the end of a sentence and a television series set in Outer Space dares to boldly split an infinitive, yet the world keeps turning. New words arrive to keep pace with changes in everyday life. The ubiquitous computer spawns *download*, *app*, *iPad* and other newcomers by the dozen. Old words find their meanings extended – a *clinch*, as well as being a romantic embrace, becomes a birdwatcher's triumph when it means 'the sighting of a rarity'. Other words pass out of fashion. It may be a loss to the language, but who nowadays, outside Scotland, where traditions die hard, uses *anent* to do the job of *about*, *regarding* or *concerning*?

Just over 100 years ago, George Bernard Shaw observed that it was impossible for an Englishman to open his mouth without making some other Englishman despise him. Shaw had accents in mind, for when he wrote *Pygmalion*, the way people spoke was a clear indication of their background, education and standing in society. The importance of pronunciation as a marker of social standing began to diminish fairly rapidly in the Sixties, though it is unlikely to vanish altogether until there is some sensational development – such as having an Archbishop of Canterbury who speaks with a

Brummie accent. Today's more pressing need is for guidance on usage, the way people choose words and string them together.

Among those offering guidance there are two schools of thought: the descriptive and the prescriptive. Those in the descriptive camp point out that English is ever-changing. Otherwise, we would still be speaking Latin, or some language even earlier. Words, they say, come in time to mean whatever the vast majority of speakers intend and use them to mean. Examples: *prevent*, which when it first came into the language meant 'precede, come before' now means 'to stop something from happening'; *prestige*, originally referring to trickery and sleight of hand, is now associated with admiration and renown; and *to resent* at one stage meant 'to show strong feelings' – even if these were feelings of gratitude.

Those in the prescriptive camp insist that the rules and conventions of language are there for a good reason: to ensure that what we say and write is exactly what we mean and will be fully understood. Relaxing the rules opens a door to confusion. If, as in some parts of the country, a boy in need of a pencil asks: 'Can I lend your pencil?' he is saying the exact opposite of what he intends. So is a politician who announces: 'We cannot underestimate the importance of clamping down on tax dodgers.'

Choose the Right Word recognises the value of both viewpoints. It explains the rules but also points out those occasions when they can safely be ignored. Careful speakers and sticklers for tradition will find sound advice on how to stay within the lines, while those who prefer their speech and writing to be more relaxed will discover when they can step outside the lines without any risk of being misunderstood – or even, if earlier attitudes return, of being despised. For example, a statement such as 'hopefully we will meet tomorrow' will raise hackles among traditionalists, but the usage is now so widespread that it has become acceptable in all but the most formal contexts. The book does not, however, hand out blanket approvals. No matter how many people think that *enormity* is a synonym for 'huge' and use it as such, this is still a mistake, at least in British English.

Oh, and one more thing. We see no reason why a work of reference should be hard work for the user. So we have tried to be entertaining as well as informative.

Robin Hosie
Vic Mayhew

Acknowledgements

The following publications and information providers were among the principal sources consulted for reference:

The Adventure of English, Melvyn Bragg (Hodder Headline); Ask Jeeves; *Between You and I – A Little Book of Bad English*, James Cochrane (Icon Books); *Bloomsbury Dictionary of Phrase and Allusion*, Nigel Rees (Bloomsbury Publishing Ltd); *Bloomsbury Good Word Guide*, edited by Martin H. Manser (Bloomsbury Publishing Ltd); *British-American Dictionary*, Norman Moss (Hutchinson); *The Cambridge Guide to English Usage*, Pam Peters (Cambridge University Press); *The Cassell Guide to Common Errors in English*, Harry Blamires (Cassell); *A Dictionary of Current English Usage* (Harrap's Reference); *A Dictionary of Modern American Usage*, H.W. Horwill (Oxford University Press); *A Dictionary of Modern English Usage*, H.W. Fowler (Oxford University Press); *Dictionary of Word Origins*, Linda and Roger Flavell (Kyle Cathie Ltd); *Fowler's Modern English Usage*, R.W. Burchfield (Oxford University Press); Google.co.uk; *How to Write and Speak Better* (Reader's Digest); *The King's English*, Kingsley Amis (Penguin Modern Classics); *Lost for Words*, John Humphrys (Hodder & Stoughton); 'Mind your language', Dot Wordsworth in *The Spectator*; *Mother Tongue*, Bill Bryson (Penguin Books); *Oxford English Dictionary* (Oxford University Press); 'Politics and the English language', George Orwell (Horizon); *The Right Word at the Right Time*, edited by John Ellison Kahn (Reader's Digest); *The Story of the English Language*, Mario Pei (George Allen & Unwin); *Strictly English*, Simon Heffer (Random House); *Success with Words* (Reader's Digest); *Troublesome Words*, Bill Bryson (Penguin Books); *U and Non-U Revisited*, edited by Richard Buckle (Debretts Peerage Ltd); *Universal Dictionary* (Reader's Digest); *The Use of English*, Randolph Quirk (Longman); Wikipedia; *Word Mysteries and Histories*, editorial staff of the American Heritage Dictionary (Houghton Mifflin); *Word Origins*, John Ayto (A. & C. Black).

a a a a A a a a a

abjure/adjure

These words are easily confused because they are so close in the written form and in sound. To avoid any error, think of their Latin prefixes: *ab-* meaning 'away' and *ad-* meaning 'towards'. In both cases, *-jure* carries the idea of a decision so serious that it carries almost the force of taking a solemn oath in court. To *abjure* strong drink, for example, is to turn away from it. And to *adjure* somebody to carry out an action is to beseech or earnestly command that person to do what you require.

accommodation

Remember when spelling this word that it has two *c*'s and two *m*'s.

accuse

It should go without saying that an accusation is not a proof. Even a notorious gossip who is accused of breaking a secret may, for once, be totally innocent. In such a case, an accuser who jumped to unjustified conclusions would be likely at the worst to face social embarrassment. But an over-hasty assumption of guilt in a matter involving criminal activity could have more serious consequences: a heavy fine or even a jail sentence. Any action or statement that is held to seriously impede or prejudice the outcome of a trial is regarded as contempt of court.

Judges take a severe view if they and their courts are held in contempt – not so severe today, however, as they did in the past. In 1949 Sylvester Bolam, editor of the *Daily Mirror*, was given a four-month prison sentence because a *Mirror* headline suggested that a man held by the police was guilty before his trial had even started. The headline was

'*Vampire – Man Held*' and the man in question was John George Haigh, who became notorious as the acid-bath murderer. He was found guilty and was sentenced to death. This did not alter the fact that Bolam was sent to prison for contempt.

AD, BC, CE

In the Western tradition, years are numbered from what is generally accepted as the birth date of Jesus. The initials AD, standing for *Anno Domini* (in the year of the Lord), are placed before the year, as in *AD 374*. BC, short for *Before Christ*, comes after the year, as in *490 BC*. If it is obvious which period the writer has in mind, there is no need to specify AD or BC: *The First World War began in 1914*.

When referring to centuries, it is not always necessary to specify AD, but if used it is placed, like BC, after the date: *The earliest known code of law dates back to Hammurabi, who became king of Babylonia in the 18th century BC. Attila the Hun, who spread terror throughout the Roman Empire in the 5th century AD, was spoken of as 'The scourge of God'. The Black Death spread misery across Europe in the 14th century*. The initials CE (*Common Era*) and BCE (*Before the Common Era*) are sometimes used by those who believe that references to AD and BC may upset non-Christians.

adequate

The word means 'sufficient for its purpose', so to describe something as *adequate enough* amounts to saying it is *sufficient enough*.

adjacent/adjoining

The distinction between these two words is sometimes blurred, which is a pity because it can be useful.

TEST YOURSELF
A. The hotel has a snooker room adjacent to/adjoining the main dining room.
B. This attractive country house, which dates from the seventeenth

century, now has an indoor swimming pool with adjacent/adjoining changing rooms.

ANSWERS
A. *Adjoining* if it is possible to walk from the dining room straight into the snooker room. *Adjacent* if the two rooms are close but not so close that you could walk out of one directly into the other.
B. *Adjoining* if the changing rooms are beside the pool. *Adjacent* if they are simply close to it.

Usage Tips

- [i] If two buildings are physically joined to each other, they are *adjoining* – handily, a word that points you in the right direction because it already contains *join*.
- [i] If two or more objects lie close together, but not so closely as to be contiguous, they are *adjacent*.

adjure *See* abjure

advertisement

The stress falls on the second syllable: *adver*isement. Shifting it to the third, and saying *advertise*ment, so that the stressed syllable rhymes with *wise*, is frowned upon in Britain. In America, *advertise*ment is the preferred pronunciation.

advise

So long as advice is given, *advise* presents no problem. But if all you are doing is passing on information, avoid such phrases as *I have to advise you*. It is enough to say *I have to tell you* – unless you are a lawyer. Lawyers and members of a few other professions tend to find that giving advice commands a higher fee than merely telling. If you want to sound official, try *I have to inform you*.

adviser/advisor

There is a widespread belief that *adviser* is the British spelling and *advisor* is American. In fact, both spellings are acceptable in both countries. *Advisor*, which is probably a back-formation from *advisory*, is gaining ground in Britain. Be aware, though, that this spelling is still disliked by traditionalists.

affect/effect

These are tiny rocks, but countless writers have stubbed a toe on them.

TEST YOURSELF

A. No matter how many times I ask my 14-year-old son to stop banging away on his drums it seems to have no affect/effect whatsoever.
B. Whatever Mary decides to do will not affect/effect Daphne's decision.
C. When Elizabeth I chastised the Earl of Essex by boxing his ears, this in affect/effect set him on the path that led to treason and ultimately to his execution.
D. The Olympic skater affected/effected a perfect double axel.
E. The soldier was put on a charge because he affected/effected a limp in an attempt to avoid guard duty.
F. This cold weather is affecting/effecting my cough.
G. Despite the evidence, many people still believe that, because of the Coriolis Affect/Effect, water always runs down the plughole clockwise in the northern hemisphere and counter-clockwise in the southern.

ANSWERS
A. *Effect* **B**. *Affect* **C**. *Effect* **D**. *Effected* **E**. *Affected* **F**. *Affecting*
G. *Effect*

Usage Tips
[i] *Effect* can be either a noun or a verb. As a noun, it means result, outcome or consequence – all of which can, when appropriate,

be used in its place. As a verb, *effect* means to perform, or bring about.

[i] *Affect*, which is almost always used as a verb, means to have an influence on, to stir the emotions or to pretend. The soldier in sample sentence **E**, for instance, was only pretending to have a limp. The adjective *affected*, meaning insincere, as in *an affected manner*, arises from this connection with pretence. The noun form of *affect* has a specialised meaning in the field of psychology.

agenda

There may still be some sticklers for tradition who believe that *agenda*, which began life as the plural of the Latin *agendum*, should remain plural and not be used in the singular. But the word is now well established as being singular, so it is fully acceptable to say, for instance: 'The meeting should not last long, since there's only one item on the agenda.' *Agenda* has even acquired a plural of its own: *agendas*. See also **data**.

ageing/aging

Both spellings are acceptable, but *ageing* is more commonly used in Britain and *aging* is standard in America.

aitch

It might save a good deal of embarrassment if English were to follow French and Italian and effectively banish the aspirated *h* from the spoken language. For the time being, though, leaving out the aspirates when voicing that 'In Hereford, Hertford and Hampshire, hurricanes hardly happen' remains a clear and usually undesirable marker of the speaker's education and upbringing. As the *Oxford English Dictionary* puts it: 'The correct treatment of initial h in speech has come to be regarded as a kind of shibboleth of social position.'

It can be just as revealing to add an *aitch* that is not meant to be pronounced – as in *hour, honour* or *honest*. There are also a few times when an initial *aitch* can be either aspirated or dropped, depending on personal preference and on which does most for the flow of a sentence. It is acceptable to speak of *a hotel* or *an hotel*, of *a historic occasion* or *an historic occasion,* to leave your horse, supposing you are rich or lucky enough to have one, in the care of *a hostler* or *an ostler.*

In the Republic of Ireland, and among Irish Catholics generally, *aitch* is pronounced *haitch* without any reflection on the social status of the speaker.

CURIO CORNER

A brief history of alcohol

Since alcohol is forbidden to Muslims it seems odd that the word had its origin among the sands of Arabia. But initially it had no connection with drink. In Arabic, *al-kohl* refers to a fine metallic powder, used to make a woman's eyes more attractive by darkening the eyelids. The word *kohl* came to be applied to other forms of powder and eventually, in the West, to liquids too. From liquids to strong drink was a short step – though, if taken too often, an unsteady one.

---

albeit

This synonym for *even though* and *although* is so rarely encountered these days outside legal documents that it is in danger of becoming archaic. This would be a pity, albeit that the word has also come to sound a little pompous.

alibi

This word's application has been extended beyond its original meaning – sometimes too far.

TEST YOURSELF

A. Sam didn't get into work yesterday but he had a good alibi: there was a strike and all the trains had stopped running.

B. The gangster rounded up potential witnesses, made them offers they couldn't refuse and coached them in what he hoped would give him an unshakeable alibi.

C. If the police call around and start asking about that break-in at No. 25, can I use you as my alibi?

D. The prosecution case collapsed after three witnesses in turn alibied the prisoner in the dock.

ANSWERS

A. *Alibi* is neither needed nor appropriate. Try *reason* or *excuse*.

B. *Alibi* is used correctly.

C. *Alibi* is acceptable, but only just.

D. *Alibi* is a noun, not a verb. Substitute … *provided alibis for* …

Usage Tips

ℹ️ Nobody can be in two different places at the same time so a convincing *alibi*, originally a Latin word conveying the message 'I was elsewhere', can provide the perfect defence against any accusation. It would be a loss to the language if this meaning were to be watered down by using the word as if it implied no more than *reason, excuse, defence* or *explanation*. Any of these would be a better choice than *alibi* in Sentence **A**.

ℹ️ The extension of *alibi* to mean the person providing one, as in Sentence **C**, just about squeezes in as being acceptable.

ℹ️ It is not acceptable in formal speech or writing to turn *alibi* into a verb, though it might be taking pedantry too far to object to such a use in everyday speech.

all right/alright

Here's a rare case of two words being better than one. Better, that is, in the sense that *all right* is generally accepted as the correct usage. It used to be said that it was not *all right* to write *alright*, but that advice is beginning to look old-fashioned. If growing numbers of people persist for long enough in what others regard as an error, the 'mistake' can shoulder aside the 'correct' version. We accept such words as *already* and *always*, goes the argument, so why baulk at *alright*? Even so, careful writers will remain loyal to the two-word spelling for some time yet.

all together/altogether

When a tug-of-war team digs in their toes and pulls as one man they are *all together*. Used as a single word, *altogether* becomes an intensifier. If the tug-of-war team wins they will be *altogether* delighted and, if their strenuous efforts lead to their collapsing in a heap, they will be *altogether* exhausted.

allusion/illusion

The first is a meaningful reference: *Some self-made men are proud of their humble origins and keep mentioning them for the sake of effect, but others resent any allusion to the poverty that drove them to strive for success.* The second is a delusion, an erroneous perception, belief or conclusion – as in *illusions of grandeur*.

almond

The first syllable is pronounced *aah*, and the full word is *aah-m'nd*. In some parts of the country, however, it is not uncommon for the *l* to be sounded: *al-m'nd*. This is acceptable as regional speech, but not as standard English.

alternate/alternative

In British English the distinction is clear enough: an *alternative* means that a choice is on offer, whereas *alternate* means taking turns. In America there is a growing tendency for the two words to be interchangeable.

TEST YOURSELF
A. Faced with an unyielding attitude on the part of management, the printers felt they had no alternative/alternate than to go on strike.
B. The driver was clearly drunk, for he was veering over to either side of the road alternatively/alternately.

C. When faced with a decision between two unappealing courses of action, there's always the third alternative/choice of doing nothing.

D. The dancers tried alternate/alternative routines in a desperate bid to impress the judges.

ANSWERS

A. *Alternative* is correct, but *than* is suspect. Say *other than* or *but.*

B. *Alternately.*

C. Careful speakers prefer *choice.*

D. *Alternative* is correct in both British and American English, although some American authorities would also allow *alternate.*

Usage Tip

ℹ️ Traditionally, an *alternative* offered a choice between no more than two possibilities. Some authorities still advise following this rule, but they appear to be fighting a losing battle. Nevertheless, if you want to avoid upsetting the traditionalists, say *choice* rather than *alternative* when faced with more than two options.

Americanisms

Henry Fowler (1858–1931), in his day and for decades afterwards an unchallengeable authority on British usage, believed that Americanisms were foreign words and should be treated as such. His brother Francis, also a prominent lexicographer, agreed and so did the overwhelming majority of the British people. There is still a lingering prejudice in Britain against importing words and phrases from the other side of the Atlantic. Yet, with the help of the powerful trio of Hollywood, TV sitcoms and pop music lyrics, many such imports find fertile soil in these islands. More often than not, British English has been enriched by American imports. And some supposed Americanisms are simply British words, returning like prodigal sons to the land of their birth.

A nation's vocabulary, arising as it does out of the experiences of its people, can provide a valuable insight into that nation's life. In America's case the picture that emerges is one of a confident, inventive, sometimes unruly nation, bent on success and living in a land full of opportunities. Words and phrases that bear out this claim include:

◆ From nature and the land: *blizzard, prairie, highway, bullfrog, rattlesnake, watershed, oxbow.*
◆ From science and invention: *telephone, bulldozer, parking meter, hydrant, bi-focals, brainstorm.*
◆ From sport and entertainment: *ballpark, fan, show business, movies, jazz, slapstick, wisecrack, sideshow, disc jockey, vaudeville, stunt, rodeo, grandstand* (when used as a verb).
◆ From the world of crime: *gangster, mobster, hoodlum, stick-up, private eye.*
◆ From food and drink: *hot dog, hamburger, cocktail, chewing gum.*
◆ From business and politics: *tycoon, credit card, jackpot, grand (1,000), gerrymander, caucus, extraordinary rendition, probe.*
◆ Words about people: *boyfriend, girlfriend, sex appeal, lipstick, teenager, dude, crank, sissy, gold-digger, highbrow, lowbrow, bogus, phoney, hefty, scrawny, rookie, maverick* (derived from the name of a Texan who rounded up unbranded cattle).
◆ Returning prodigals: *Fall (Autumn), cabin, guess (in the sense of suppose), reckon (suppose), quit, raise (children).*

A number of Americanisms have established themselves in the British vocabulary without ousting the British incumbents. When elections come round, some politicians will *stand* for office, in the traditional way, while others will *run*, in the more energetic-sounding American style. The British *lorry* shares our roads with the American *truck*. The expression *No way!* no longer sounds strange to British ears. A football player who puts on a flamboyant show to invite applause and adulation after scoring a goal may well be accused of *grandstanding*.

A considerably larger number of American words have so far failed to establish a foothold in Britain. When it comes to personal transport, as distinct from commercial, our motorists are so patriotic that they might as well be waving flags. Their luggage, golf clubs and spare wheels are stored in a *boot*, not in a *trunk*. The noise of their car's engine is quietened by a *silencer*, not a *muffler*. They polish the *wings*, not the *fenders*. When they fill up – those who can afford to do so, that is – *petrol* goes into their tanks, not *gasoline*. Passengers on a rail journey depend on the alertness of the *train driver* not the *engineer*, and air travellers, showing varying degrees of weariness and impatience, *wait in a queue* rather than *stand in line*.

Outside the house, we walk on *pavements*, not *sidewalks* and shop at a *chemist's* not a *druggist's*. At home, babies' *nappies* are changed, not their *diapers*. Young boys wear short *trousers* rather than *knee pants*, and munch *biscuits*, not *cookies*. At breakfast they will spread *jam* on their bread, not *jelly*. For *jelly*, not *jello*, is a special treat at children's parties. And the wobblier the better.

Houses in Britain have *post codes*, not *zip codes*. Friends keep in touch on *mobile phones*, not *cell phones*. The last letter of the alphabet is pronounced *zed*, not *zee*, and what is sometimes referred to as the smallest room in the house is the *toilet*, the *lavatory* or the *loo*, not the *washroom* or the *bathroom*.

Most of us feel comfortable with the language we began to learn at our mothers' knees, then spoke, heard and in many cases read every day as we were growing up. This explains why British attitudes towards Americanisms are determined largely by age.

These attitudes fall into three main groups: the die-in-the-last-ditch traditionalists; the go-with-the-flow middle-of-the-roaders; and the cutting-edge trendies. The traditionalists see no reason why a good British word or phrase should be jostled aside by an American upstart. Nobody likes to lose a job, but if this happens a last-ditch defender prefers *you're sacked* to *you're fired* and would squirm at the expression *we're going to have to let you go*. Members of this group pull back disdainfully if they hear somebody use *hopefully* in its disputed sense – as in *hopefully, we will still be batting at close of play*. And they would never dream of calling a *cockerel* a *rooster*, or the lavatory a *restroom* or *bathroom*.

The middle-of-the-roaders, who are by far the largest group, accept some Americanisms without demur, reject a fair number and use others only sparingly. They are highly likely, for instance, to accept the disputed use of *hopefully* and, following the American pronunciation, to stress the second syllable and say *har**ass*** rather than the British ***har**ass*.

American spelling changes – *humor* instead of *humour*, *center* in preference to *centre* and so on – have had little impact in Britain, even among those in the third group, who like to keep up with new trends and to use language that is on the edge of being experimental. Young people are most likely to be found in this group, and they often take their cue from America. They will address a male-female group, or even one composed entirely of females, as '*You guys*'. They have adapted a tee-shirt slogan that shows a red heart between the words *I* and *New York* by turning the heart, a symbol of *love,* into a word. A girl might say to her friend: '*I heart* your new shoes'. Another example of this new way of speaking comes from American television: 'I'm loving this kind of music' instead of 'I love this kind of music'. If you are looking for a trendy-sounding way of indicating that you are not much concerned about a topic, one way or the other, throw in an occasional *whatever*.

What of the future? The only guide we have is what happened in the past. When the English language began to spread around the world, carried by sailors, traders, pirates, adventurers and religious communities looking for greater freedom, it was a language spoken by perhaps seven million people. Today an estimated 750 million speak English as a first or second language. One reason for this success is that English is seen as a passport to a better life. It is the language of wealth and power. In the late 19th and early 20th centuries the role of the world's richest and most influential power began to pass from the United Kingdom to the United States. And American English flourished. Nothing illustrates this point more clearly than the shift in the meaning of the word *billion*. British dictionaries of the 1980s defined it as meaning 1,000,000 million, while giving a somewhat condescending nod to those across the Atlantic who took it to mean, as it did in France,

1,000 million. Today it is agreed in Britain and the entire world that a *billion* is 1,000 million. Any doubts about its meaning would cause confusion in every classroom and chaos in every stock market.

This does not mean that British English is under any serious threat. The language of Shakespeare, Dickens, Jane Austen, Evelyn Waugh and George Orwell has always been vigorous enough to absorb words from outside. And to benefit from so doing.

CURIO CORNER

Running amok

Newspaper editors of the old school used to insist that only a Malay could run *amok*. It was, after all, a Malay word, describing a warrior who swung his double-edged *kris* in a frenzy as he did his best to rid the world of his enemies. There are not many opportunities these days to swing a *kris* or to use *amok* in its original sense. This means that the old restriction is now looked upon as endearingly pedantic. *Amok* is such a useful way of suggesting something that is wild and out of control that it can even be used in turbulent financial times to describe the behaviour of the stock market.

and (at the start of a sentence)

Tireless and earnest efforts by generations of schoolteachers to suppress the habit of starting a sentence with *And* have failed because there are no sound arguments to support them. If anybody tries to tell you otherwise, gently point out that Genesis, the first book of the Bible, owes much of its literary power to the piling of *And* upon *And*. Or quote the opening lines of William Blake's *Jerusalem*:

> *And did those feet, in ancient time*
> *Walk upon England's mountains green?*

anything

The word ends with a *g,* not with a *k,* but even on the BBC it has been mispronounced as *anythink.* See also **something**.

apostrophe

This speck of a punctuation mark has been known to create a mountain of problems. Most of the mistakes arise because it is fairly easy to muddle up its two main purposes. An apostrophe can either indicate possession or show that a letter or number has been omitted.

TEST YOURSELF

A. It's/Its a long way to Tipperary.

B. Its/It's been ages since we last sat down for a chat.

C. The show isn't/isnt over until the fat lady sings.

D. Be gentle with that horse when you bandage it's/its leg.

E. Who's/whose turn is it to make the tea – yours/your's or mine?

F. If your friends can't/cant take my advice, the loss will be theirs/ their's.

G. The Cold War lasted from the late 1940's/1940s well into the 1980's/1980s.

H. Back in '82/82 I was down on my luck but I've/Ive picked up since then.

I. The tattoo on Lewis's/Lewis' forearm proclaimed his undying love for Susan, but unfortunately his wife's name was Geraldine.

J. The children's/childrens' new football jerseys made them look extremely smart at the kick-off.

K. This handy book lists all the do's and don'ts/does and donts of DIY.

L. There is no point in bankrupting ourselves, just to keep up with the Jones's/Joneses.

M. Best prices in the market for apple's/apples, tomatoe's/tomatoes and new potato's/potatoes.

ANSWERS

A. *It's.*

B. *It's.*

C. *Isn't.*

D. *Its.*

E. *Whose* and *yours.*

F. *Can't* and *theirs.*

G. *1940s* and *1980s.*

H. *'82* and *I've.*

I. *Lewis's.*

J. *Children's.*

K. *Do's* and *don'ts.*

L. *Joneses.*

M. *Apples, tomatoes and new potatoes.*

Usage Tips – When to use the apostrophe and when to leave it out

Missing letters or figures

[i] One of the main jobs of the apostrophe is to indicate that a letter or a figure has been missed out. *It is* and *it has* both become *it's; I am* becomes *I'm; you have* is contracted to *you've; you are* to *you're; how is* becomes *how's;* and so on. It is not usually advisable to use such contractions if a formal tone is required.

[i] As with letters, so with figures. To write *The Beatles revolutionised pop music in the '60s* is correct not only because it is true but also because the number *19*, indicating the century, has been omitted. To write *The 1960's saw the emergence of the Beatles* is incorrect because no figures are missing. A plain *1960s* is all that is needed. Be especially watchful in the case of *its*. This three-letter pronoun causes far more than its share of bewilderment, but the rule is simple: *it's* is the right choice only when it's short for *it is* or *it has*.

Possession

[i] The other main job of the apostrophe is to convey the idea of possession – as in *the dog's dinner* or *my grandfather's clock*. Problems arise when the possessive apostrophe and the 'missing letter' apostrophe are confused.

🚹 The pronouns *my, mine, your, yours, his, her, hers, our, ours, their, theirs* and *whose* already carry the notion of possession, and so need no apostrophe. Frequently, but mistakenly, one is allocated to them. *Yours* is mistakenly written as *your's, ours* becomes *our's, hers* is written as *her's, theirs* as *their's,* and *whose* as *who's*. An apostrophe is necessary, however, when *who's* is short for *who is*.

Singulars and plurals

🚹 When used with a singular noun the apostrophe comes in front of the *s,* as in *the cat's whiskers* or *the girl's doll*.

🚹 With plural nouns that end with an *s,* the apostrophe comes after the *s,* as in *the workers' pay claim*.

🚹 Not all plurals end with an *s – children,* for example. In such cases, use an *apostrophe s* to indicate possession: *the children's party*.

🚹 If a singular noun ends in *s,* as in *genius,* the apostrophe indicating possession is placed after the *s,* then a second *s* is added, as in *the genius's latest invention*.

Names

🚹 If a name ends in *s* the sound of the spoken word is often a trustworthy guide to where to place the apostrophe: *St James's Park*.

🚹 Some authorities believe that one *s* is better than two, and possibly more elegant. They prefer Charles *Dickens'* sense of humour to Charles *Dickens's*. Usually, either choice is fully acceptable. The most important exceptions are set out below.

🚹 Names from ancient history usually follow the *one-s* convention, so it's *Achilles' heel* and *Pythagoras' theorem*. This also applies to the name of Jesus: *Jesus' parables*.

🚹 While it pays to follow the advice just given, people, companies and organisations of any kind have the right to spell their names and place apostrophes how and where they please. In the London area, three Church of England schools within a reasonable distance of one another call themselves *St James's, St James'* and *St James.* There is a St Andrews Close in Ruislip and a St Andrew's Close in Staines. *Walkers' crisps* looks like a tastier choice than *Walkers's crisps* – though the manufacturers have avoided the problem by not having any apostrophe on the packet.

[i] *Mind your p's and q's.* The apostrophe is also sometimes used simply to add clarity – as, for example in *p's and q's, do's and don'ts, but me no but's* and *four 9's are 36.*

CURIO CORNER

The greengrocer's apostrophe

An unwanted apostrophe that tries to sneak in under the guise of forming a plural is widely known – and derided – as *the greengrocer's apostrophe.* Those who care for the language have pointed an accusing finger at greengrocers who offer for sale *apple's, potato's, tomato's, cauliflower's, swede's* and so on. Whether or not greengrocers were the first offenders, the error has now spread far beyond their trade. In just about any high street you may walk into shops that offer to process *digital photo's,* or to supply *boxes of tool's.* One alert apostrophe-watcher came across a car showroom that drew attention to its stock of *Honda's.* The unforgettable Keith Waterhouse, journalist, novelist and playwright, was so disturbed and so amused by the snowstorm of apostrophes falling to earth where they were not needed that he founded the AAAA – the Association for the Abolition of the Aberrant Apostrophe. A brave attempt, but the malady lingers on.

artefact/artifact

In Britain the spelling is *artefact* – taking a cue from the Latin *arte* ('by skill'). In the USA the word is spelled *artifact.*

as

This simple word is surrounded by pitfalls for the unwary. See how many you can avoid.

TEST YOURSELF

A. If you feel as tired as me, why don't we stop dancing and sit the next one out?

B. As far as having a flawless sense of timing, there are very few comics today who could come anywhere near Jack Benny in his prime.

C. There is no shortage of food writers eager to point out that chicken does not taste as good as it used to.

D. John picked up the phone as his wife was taking a shower.

E. I'm beginning to think that you dislike Sheila as much as Jane.

F. According to one of their coaches, some of the training sessions for the Welsh rugby team have been as tough, if not tougher than, an actual game.

G. There wasn't a tennis player in the entire county who could hit a backhand shot as sweetly as she.

H. As from today there will be no more smoking on the steps outside the main door.

ANSWERS

A. Strictly speaking, *as tired as me* should be *as tired as I*. In informal speech or writing, however, *as tired as me* is acceptable.

B. A thought that begins *As far as* ... is only half a thought until it is completed by *is concerned* or some similar phrase.

C. No problems here – apart, perhaps, from what has happened to the taste of chickens.

D. Ambiguous. Did John pick up the phone *while* his wife was in the shower or *because* she was there?

E. Ambiguity has crept in again. Does the person being addressed dislike Sheila as much as she dislikes Jane or as much as Jane does?

F. A second *as* is needed. The training sessions were *as tough as* an actual game.

G. The *she* may sound pretentious but grammatically it is impeccable.

H. The opening *as* is redundant. All that is needed is a simple *From today…*

Usage Tips

[i] *As tired as me*, in Sentence **A**, sounds natural and is acceptable in everyday speech, but it is grammatically incorrect. To be sure of choosing the right pronoun after *as*, try mentally adding the missing verb: *as tired as I am* – or, in Sentence **G**, *as sweetly as she could*.

[i] Comparisons that begin with *as far as* need to be completed with *is concerned, are concerned* or even a simple *goes*. If doing so makes the sentence sound inelegant, consider rewriting it entirely. Sentence **B**, for instance, might read: *Jack Benny had such a flawless sense of timing that few comics today could come anywhere near him in his prime.*

[i] Be on guard against ambiguity when using *as*. You may need to rephrase a sentence. The meaning of Sentence **E**, for example, would be clear if it spelled things out: *I'm beginning to think that you dislike Sheila as much as Jane does* – unless, of course, what you mean is: *I'm beginning to think that you dislike Sheila as much as you dislike Jane.*

ask (a big ask)

Few provocations will send a traditionalist reaching for his revolver faster than a noun masquerading as a verb – unless, as in *a big ask*, it's a verb that tries to pass itself off as a noun. The phrase originated as a lively addition to the vocabulary of sports commentators. But a whiff of the charlatan hangs around its use outside sport. Safe alternatives are *a big thing to ask, a big/tough question to ask,* or simply *a big question.*

authoritative/authoritive/authoritarian

There is, as yet, no such word as *authoritive*, although a surprisingly large number of people seem to think there is. Dictionary compilers have so far refused to grant it an entry visa, but their attitude may change if its popularity continues to grow apace. The right word for a leader who has a commanding presence is either *authoritative* or *authoritarian*. The difference between these two is that in the first case the leader's authority is acknowledged and freely accepted whereas in the second case it is resented because it is backed by force or threats.

awesome

If ever a word has earned the right to be put out to grass, this must be it. When the dictionary defines *awe* it uses such words as reverence, dread, wonder, majestic and sublime. A tennis player's backhand, no matter how many championships it may win, cannot accurately be described as *awesome.* Nor can the speed at which a car accelerates from 0 to 60 mph, or even the food served at a Michelin-starred restaurant. If *awesome* and *awe-inspiring* lose their impact through being overused, what words are left to describe the Pyramids or the Sydney Opera House? To ring the changes, try *impressive, remarkable, extraordinary, eye-catching,* even *sensational.*

b b 𝕓 ⠃ B b 𝕭 b b

backing into sentences

What's wrong with the following sentences?

TEST YOURSELF

A. As a leading member of the Opposition, it surprises me to find that you support the Government's proposal to increase taxes.

B. Like everything else on the shelves, Jenny found the biscuits were well past their sell-by date.

C. Abandoned by the roadside, John found a rusty old car that had been stripped of its number plates.

D. Having tried one feeble excuse after another, Dorothy was fairly certain that James would not get away with shifting the blame this time.

E. 'Openly gay, he was perhaps happiest when out riding one of his motorcycles' (*Daily Telegraph*).

F. As a long-term sufferer from body odour, I wonder if you would care to try this new and remarkably effective roll-on freshener.

G. 'Then a bachelor, my fridge at home was obviously empty' (*Daily Telegraph*).

ANSWERS

A. The person who is surprised is not, whatever the sentence suggests, a leading member of the Opposition.

B. It was the biscuits that were on the shelves, not Jenny.

C. John was not abandoned by the roadside. The car was.

D. The serial excuse-maker was James, but backing into the sentence switches the blame to Dorothy.

E. No evidence is offered in support of the notion that there is a link between owning more than one motorbike and being gay.

F. The long-term sufferer from body odour is the person being addressed – not, as the sentence suggests, the one trying to be helpful.

G. Can a fridge be a bachelor?

Usage Tips

📄 Every writer who backs into a sentence has, knowingly or not, fallen under the spell of Latin. The Ancient Romans, who were partial to this construction, did not need to concern themselves too deeply about the sequence of words in a sentence because key words in Latin carry suffixes, prefixes and other signals that reveal the part they play. In English, by contrast, the position of a word can be critical – showing, for instance, what is the subject of a sentence and what is its object. If you back into a sentence, the subject will almost always be the first noun or pronoun that follows the opening phrase. In Sentence **C**, for instance, John is the noun closest to the opening phrase, suggesting that he, rather than the rusty car, has been abandoned by the roadside.

📄 The easiest way to avoid being misunderstood is to avoid backing into sentences in the first place. The ambiguity vanishes from Sentence **A**, for instance, if it is rewritten as: *Since you are a leading member of the Opposition, it surprises me to find that you are in favour of the government's proposal to increase taxes.*

📄 If you must back into a sentence, how can you do so safely? Simply make sure that the first noun or pronoun following the opening phrase is also the subject of the sentence. Sentence **G**, for example, might read: *Since I was then a bachelor, I knew that my fridge at home would be empty.* This rephrasing may not be elegant but at least it is clear.

ℹ️ Hanging participles, dangling clauses and misrelated constructions are all among the terms used to describe mistakes made by backing into sentences.

bail out/bale out

Which should it be?

TEST YOURSELF

A. With both engines gone and the cockpit on fire, the pilot had no choice but to bale out/bail out.

B. Bail/bale is unlikely to be granted if the police believe that an accused man would try to flee the country.

C. If the waves get any bigger and we start shipping water, then start baling/bailing at top speed.

D. Jeremy is deeply in debt because of his losses at poker and he has no rich friends to bale/bail him out.

E. Thousands of bales/bails of wool piled up at the dockside during the strike.

ANSWERS

A. *Bale out* (British). *Bail out* (US).

B. *Bail.*

C. *Baling* (British). *Bailing* (American but increasingly acceptable in British English).

D. *Bail him out.*

E. *Bales.*

Usage Tips

ℹ️ The Old French word *bailler* means to lock somebody up; so a prisoner who is released on the security that cash that will be forfeited if he fails to turn up for trial is *bailed out*.

ℹ️ The Middle English word *baille* (bucket) gave rise to the expression *bail* for the act of scooping water from a boat. In Britain this spelling was shouldered aside by *bale* but it is beginning to make a comeback. Either spelling is acceptable, with *bale* preferred by traditionalists.

[i] When an individual, a bank or some other commercial concern is in trouble and needs a cash injection, the operation in both British and American English is known as *bailing out*.

[i] A bale is a large tied bundle, usually of wool or straw, and this meaning is recalled in the idea of a pilot *baling out* of an aeroplane – perhaps because the action resembles tossing a bundle out of the plane. This spelling, however, is only for Britons. An American pilot faced with an emergency will have to decide whether or not to *bail out*.

baited/bated

Even the normally impeccable *Spectator* magazine can go wrong. An article about Barack Obama, shortly after he became America's 44th President, stated: 'Now everyone waits with baited breath for the new Prez to pull the rabbit out of the hat.' Not unless they were reeking of garlic they didn't. Breath that is held back, in anticipation or excitement, is *bated,* not *baited.* Think of *abate*, 'to reduce or diminish'.

begging the question

It is a common mistake to believe that *begging the question* means no more than to make a statement that raises a question in the listener's mind. Question-begging certainly raises a question, but it does so in a particular way – by assuming that what is stated is self-evidently true. It is begging the question, for instance, to say that an accused man must be guilty, because otherwise the police would not have arrested him.

behove/behoove

Either spelling and either pronunciation (*-hove* as in rove or *-hoove* as in move) is acceptable, depending on who and where you are. British speakers say *it behoves us* and Americans say *it behooves us.*

belly

There is a tendency to shy away from this word, which is seen as being slightly vulgar, and to prefer terms from the same area of the body – *stomach* or *tummy*. These euphemisms do not mean exactly the same as *belly*, but their meaning is clear. When *belly* is coupled with other words it seems to take a step up the social ladder. *Belly laugh*, *belly button*, *belly dancer* and *bellyflop* all still have a slight air of cheerful vulgarity but there are no inhibitions about their use.

between you and I

To some minds, *between you and I* sounds more well-bred than *between you and me*. But, like *from you and I*, and *to you and I*, it is a grammatical howler.

TEST YOURSELF
A. We were given book tokens for Christmas but between you and I/ me, neither of us is much of a reader.
B. At a corporate polo afternoon a few years ago I bumped into the BBC's Andrew Neil and asked if he'd like to accompany my wife and I to a grandstand view of the afternoon's decisive chukka (newspaper article).
C. My wife and I/me usually leave our Christmas presents wrapped until the children have opened theirs.
D. The dog with the red collar is the one that ran off with the ball when Geoff and I/me were playing in the park.
E. This card comes with lots of love from Peggy and I/me.
F. The best way you could make amends to Charles and I/me would be to offer a sincere apology.

ANSWERS
A. *You and me.*
B. *My wife and me.* Polo may be the sport of princes and playboys, but that does not confer the right to sound like a grammatical pauper.
C. *My wife and I.*
D. *Geoff and I.*
E. *Peggy and me.*

F. *Charles and me.*

Usage Tips

ℹ️ The pronouns *I, we, he, she* and *they* are always the subjects of any sentence or phrase in which they appear – that is, they perform the action indicated by the verb. In Sentence **C**, for example, the main verb is *leave* and my *wife and I* are the subjects who leave the presents. The pronouns *me, him, her, us* and *them* are the objects of a verb. Things happen to them. In Sentence **B** *my wife and me* are the objects of the verb *accompany*. Think of the subjects of a sentence as being like actors on the stage, and the objects as being like the audience for whom the action is performed.

ℹ️ If your grammar is a little rusty, an easy way to sort out subjects from objects is to check whether the pronoun sounds right when it stands alone. You would not say *This present comes with lots of love from I* or *You didn't give we much notice*. Not unless you were trying to assume a regional dialect. Nor would you say *Me leave my presents wrapped*.

ℹ️ Another tip is that *between* is always followed by *me* rather than *I*. Those who say *between you and I* lay themselves open to the charge of trying to sound genteel.

ℹ️ Some authorities maintain that *between you and I* is now so widely used, and has such a long pedigree, that it has become acceptable. Careful speakers shudder at the thought.

CURIO CORNER

Shakespeare breaks the 'between you and I' rule

Those who, for whatever reason, say *between you and I* are in better company than they may know. Shakespeare, in *The Merchant of Venice*, has one of his characters say: 'All debts are cleared between you and I.' But Shakespeare earned the right to make his own rules, and in any case the language has moved on since his day.

bi- (biannual, biennial, bicentennial, bi-weekly, bi-monthly)

The Latin prefix *bi-* can mean either double or a half. Is a bi-weekly newspaper, for example, published twice a week or once every two weeks? If there is any possibility of doubt in such cases it is a good idea to add a signpost – as in *The bi-weekly* Rochdale Observer, *an ornament of provincial publishing, comes out on Wednesdays and Saturdays.*

A great deal of possible confusion about the meaning of *bi-* has been dispelled by the development of some useful conventions. *Biannual* means twice a year, *biennial* means every two years and *bicentennial* means every 200 years. A *biennial* plant flowers and produces fruit in two years, whereas a *perennial* lives on from year to year. The United States celebrated its *bicentenary*, the 200th anniversary of the Declaration of Independence, in 1976.

CURIO CORNER

The delightful Miss Belinda Blurb

When his publishers decided to throw a party for booksellers and send their guests home with a free copy of his latest book, the American humourist Gelet Burgess took up the proposal eagerly. Since he was also an illustrator they asked him to create the cover too. Burgess produced a short, entertaining text, placing above it the illustration of a delightfully attractive girl to whom he gave the name Belinda Blurb. That was in 1906, since when the word *blurb* has caught on, with the meaning of a brief publicity notice, especially one that appears on the flap of a book jacket.

bored

You can be tired of waiting or fed up of waiting, but unless you want to associate yourself with below-standard English you cannot be *bored of* waiting. The correct choice is either *bored by* or *bored with*. Somehow, *of* has insinuated itself in recent years, and this is not a development to be encouraged.

CURIO CORNER

The ordeal of Captain Boycott

Captain Charles Cunningham Boycott was a land agent in County Mayo at a time when impoverished Irish peasants, living in cottages that were tied to their jobs, were agitating for tenants' rights. His job was to carry out the orders of the landowner, Lord Erne, and make sure that the tenants paid their rents on time and in full. In 1880, following an exceptionally poor harvest, the tenants asked for a rent reduction of 25%. Lord Erne refused this demand, saying he could only afford to give up 10%.

This brought him into the front line of a dispute between Parliament, which laid down the laws under which Ireland was governed, and the Irish leader Charles Stewart Parnell, an inspired orator who happened to be of Protestant stock. In one of his most brilliant speeches Parnell advised tenants not to take up arms against oppression but to use a new weapon: total isolation of the oppressor.

There soon came a chance to try it out. When Lord Erne's tenants refused to pay what he was charging, he sent in Boycott to collect the money. Eight tenants refused to consider paying, so the Captain served them with eviction notices. The response was swift. Shopkeepers refused to sell food to Boycott, the postman refused to deliver his letters, nobody would wash his shirts and all his servants walked out. As for Lord Erne, his crops were waiting in the fields but nobody was prepared to harvest them. Finally he had to bring in labourers from the predominantly Protestant northern counties to do the work, protected by massive numbers of armed guards. Captain Boycott and his family stuck out isolation for a year, then left Ireland for ever. Perhaps his greatest mistake was to write to *The Times,* complaining about his treatment. The publicity this generated made his name a byword in just about every language. Any oppressive or unjust regime that seems to offer no hope to its people risks being faced with a boycott.

both

Apart from being ill-mannered and inviting painful retribution, what's wrong with walking up to two men in a pub and announcing: 'I could beat *the both* of you with one hand tied behind my back'? The answer is that as well as being rude and provocative, it is also an offence against grammar. The word *the* is redundant. The correct usage is either *I could beat both of you* or *I could beat the pair of you.*

burglary

It used to be the case that the police or a householder could bring a charge of *burglary* only if a felony had been committed by night. Now, however, the time of day is not material. Burglary is breaking into a house or any other building, at any time, with the intention of stealing, causing injury or criminal damage or committing rape. See also **robbery**.

burned/burnt

The day may come when British usage falls into line with American, but until then it is as well to know the difference.

TEST YOURSELF
A. A burned/burnt child fears the fire.
B. The fire-cracker exploded too soon and a 14-year-old boy was badly burnt/burned.
C. Cortes burnt/burned his boats at Vera Cruz, so the story goes, so that his soldiers would not be able to turn back from his invasion of the Aztec empire.
D. The novelist had a prodigious memory, so he did not despair when his housekeeper carelessly burned/burnt the manuscript of his latest book on the sitting room fire.
E. The bonfire burnt/burned all night long and is still smouldering.
F. I see you've burnt/burned the toast again.

ANSWERS
A. *Burnt.*

B. *Burnt* (British) *Burned* (US).

C. *Burned*.

D. *Burned*.

E. *Burned*.

F. *Burnt*.

Usage Tips

- [i] In British English, *burnt* is the usual choice if the burning has been completed: *The house burnt to the ground*. When the burning is incomplete, as in Sentence **E**, *burned* is preferred.

- [i] When the word is used as an adjective, it is usually spelled *burnt* – as in *burnt toast, a burnt offering*, and so on. Americans use *burnt* as an adjective but otherwise prefer *burned*.

but

Forget the so-called rule. There is no sound reason why you should not use *But* at the start of a sentence. After all, Shakespeare did. But don't overdo it, or you may become monotonous. As an alternative, try an occasional *however*. But not too often, or you may come to sound stiff and over-formal.

C C C C **C** C C C C

When every candidate was whiter than white

An Ancient Roman standing for public office would wear a dazzling white toga at election time, as a token that he was spotlessly pure. The Latin for white is *candidus* and somebody who donned the white toga was a *candidatus*. Hence our word *candidate*, and our expectation that those putting themselves forward for public office should be *candid* when they make promises at election time.

cannon/canon

The one-n *canon* is a clergyman or a body of law, usually governing church matters. The two-n *cannon* is a gun.

canvas/canvass

The one-s *canvas* refers to various types of fabric, used to make tents and sails, or as a surface for artists to paint on. The two-s canvass means 'to solicit votes' – a task that may sometimes be made easier by a fabrication or two.

Celtic

With one notable exception the word is pronounced **Kel**tik. Every football fan knows the exception. The Scottish team Celtic is pronounced **Sel**tik – a fact worth remembering if you visit Glasgow.

cheers

Using *cheers* as a substitute for *thank you* is trendy and encountered most often among younger people, but is frowned upon by many in that age cohort, as well as by most of the older generation.

CURIO CORNER

The perils of checkmate

In chess, a game that reached the West from Persia (Iran), victory belongs to the player who puts an opponent's king in *checkmate*. The word is derived from the Persian *shah mat* – 'the king is dead'. But in truth the game does not end with the king's death. It is won or lost when he is captured. In ancient Persia this meant, in all likelihood, that he was as good as dead.

---

chronic

Avoid, if you can, using this word to mean something that is overpoweringly bad. *The way you conducted yourself last night was something chronic* is slang – and what is worse, slang that is going out of fashion. *Chronic* has a precise medical meaning, referring to a disease that is long-standing and is likely to recur. A disease that comes on suddenly, by contrast, is termed *acute*. It is legitimate, by extension, to speak of a *chronic* lack of understanding or a *chronic* economic problem and so on.

classic/classical

Both words convey the notion of something that is at or near to the top of its class, but in different ways.

TEST YOURSELF
A. It was a classic/classical case of misunderstanding – the police arrested the wrong man.
B. Which do you prefer – classic/classical music or jazz?
C. My daughter gave me a DVD of pop classics/classicals of the Seventies for my birthday.

D. Eve eclipsed all rivals when she swept down the staircase wearing her classic/classical Yves Saint Laurent dress.

E. The majority of our schools no longer give their pupils a thorough grounding in the works of the classic/classical authors.

ANSWERS
A. *Classic* **B.** *Classical* **C.** *Classics* **D.** *Classic* **E.** *Classical*

Usage Tips

[i] Anything that is acknowledged as being at or near the top of its class, from a joke to a golf swing, may be described as *classic*. *Classical* has a more limited range of meanings. It is applied most often to the art, architecture and literature of ancient Greece and Rome – and sometimes to those of other bygone civilisations.

[i] In music, *classical* is usually taken to refer to the works of the great masters: Bach, Mozart, Beethoven, Wagner, Shostakovitch, Mahler, Ravel, Britten and so on.

complement/compliment

Estate agents and food-and-wine experts seem to be among the groups most in danger of confusing these two.

TEST YOURSELF

A. The venison is complimented/complemented by chestnuts on a bed of red cabbage.

B. That was a superb meal! My compliments/complements to the chef.

C. Jane took Henry's proposal as a great complement/compliment but said that since he already had a wife, she could not marry him.

D. Lucky you! You have won two complementary/complimentary seats to the men's finals at Wimbledon.

E. The house is complimented/complemented by an attractive walled garden.

F. 'This wine finishes with delicate silky tannins and is further complimented by vanillan oak' (label on a bottle of Australian wine).

ANSWERS

A. *Complemented*   **B**. *Compliments*   **C**. *Compliment*
D. *Complimentary*   **E**. *Complemented*   **F**. *Complemented*

Usage Tips

ℹ️ To *compliment* means 'to praise'. In Sentence **A** the chestnuts could not *compliment* the venison unless they had the power of speech. In Sentence **B** the chef is being praised, and in Sentence **C** Jane takes a proposal as a form of praise.

ℹ️ *Complimentary* can also mean *free of charge*, and this is the meaning intended in Sentence **D**.

ℹ️ To *complement* something means 'to accompany and complete'. In Sentence **E**, the garden completes the property being offered for sale.

composed of/comprising

Both words refer to the parts that make up a whole, which explains why they are often confused.

TEST YOURSELF

A. Our team had no chance. It was comprised of/composed of players who had never learned to kick a ball with both feet.

B. The tool kit comprises/is composed of a hammer, nails, a saw and five screwdrivers.

C. This jam has an odd taste. It seems to be comprised of/composed of just about anything but fruit.

D. The Westminster Parliament comprises/is composed of two Houses: the Commons and the Lords.

E. The orchestra was somewhat unusual, in that it was comprised/composed entirely of saxophone players.

ANSWERS

A. *Composed of.*

B. Both are correct, with a slight preference for *comprises* because it refers to a list of practical items.

C. *Composed of.*

D. Both are correct, with a slight preference for *is composed of* because it refers to human beings.

E. *Composed of.*

Usage Tips

ℹ️ The word *of* sits happily when it follows *composed* but it should never be used after *comprised*. This is because *comprised* means 'consisting of, made up of'. To say *comprised of* amounts to saying *of of*.

ℹ️ Even acknowledged masters of prose can slip up, especially in long sentences: '… students who came from families where they were neglected or abused and thus grades one through six, for Homer Wells, were comprised of experiences that were more combative than educational' (John Irving, *The Cider House Rules*).

CURIO CORNER

The long journey of comrades

The word *comrade* comes from the Latin *camera* 'a room', which in turn derives from the Greek *kamara*, 'a vault'. It came into Spanish as *camarada*, 'a room-mate' who was likely in bygone days to be a fellow soldier. And who would be more likely to be chosen as a room-mate than a friend?

continual/continuous

Watch out for the important difference between these two.

TEST YOURSELF

A. I couldn't get a wink of sleep last night because of the continuous/continual rows between the couple in the flat upstairs.

B. A continuous/continual white line along the edge of the road means that parking is either prohibited or restricted.

C. Sally lay in the meadow, dozing off to the continuous/continual droning of the bees.

D. Once you start borrowing from loan sharks you'll find your debts continuously/continually rising, to the point where you might even lose your house.

E. Our brave little boat battled its way through the continuous/continual rise and fall of mountainous waves.

ANSWERS

A. *Continual*   **B.** *Continuous*   **C.** *Continuous*   **D.** *Continually*

E. Either word could be correct, depending on how you define a wave.

Usage Tips

ℹ️ An activity that repeatedly stops then starts again is continual. In Sentence **A**, for example, the reference to rows, rather than a single row, makes *continual* the right choice, since the arguing kept stopping then starting again.

ℹ️ An activity or anything else that goes on for a long time without interruption or pause is continuous. In Sentence **B** the white line is unbroken, so *continuous* is the right choice.

ℹ️ Sometimes, depending on your standpoint, either word may be appropriate. If you think of waves as including troughs as well as peaks, their rise and fall is unbroken, making *continuous* the right choice in Sentence **E**. If you count only the peaks, then the word is *continual* because the peaks rise then fall away.

convince/persuade

The two are synonyms, and both mean 'to induce somebody to believe something'. But they are not always interchangeable.

TEST YOURSELF

A. It took Michael more than a year, but he finally convinced his wife to give up smoking.

B. It took Michael more than a year, but he finally persuaded his wife to give up smoking.

C. I don't find your theory that dogs always come to look like their owners to be entirely persuasive/convincing.

ANSWERS

A. Incorrect. If *convinced* is used, the sentence should be along the lines of: *It took Michael more than a year, but he finally convinced his wife that it would be a good idea for her to give up smoking.*

B. Correct.

C. Either word is suitable.

Usage Tips

ℹ️ To *convince* is to change somebody's mind, whereas to *persuade* leads to a change in behaviour, as well as in attitudes and ideas.

CURIO CORNER

The island of copper

The reddish-brown metal copper, so much in demand today because it is an excellent conductor of electricity, was even more highly prized in the world of Ancient Rome. For when alloyed with tin it made brass, and brass was used to make weapons, armour, tools, statues and many household items. The Romans drew the vast bulk of their copper supplies from the island they called Cyprium – modern Cyprus – so it comes as no surprise that they called the metal *cyprium aes*, 'the metal of Cyprus'. With a slight shift the Latin name became *cuprum*, a clear ancestor of *copper*.

could have/should have/might have/would have

It is a sign of sloppiness to say or write *of* instead of *have*. The mistake probably arose because *have,* when spoken, can sound very close to *of*, especially when it is contracted, as in *I could've danced all night.*

credible/credulous

The two are sometimes confused – as are their opposites, *incredible* and *incredulous*.

TEST YOURSELF

A. That story of Peter's about how he tackled five thugs and put them to flight is simply incredulous/incredible.

B. Call me a credible/credulous old fool, but I don't think it's in Peter's nature to lie about his exploits.

C. He may not intend to lie, but so many of the stories he tells are simply incredible/incredulous.

ANSWERS

A. *Incredible*   **B.** *Credulous*   **C.** *Incredible*

Usage Tip

[i] *Credible* means 'believable', whereas *credulous* describes somebody who believes too readily.

CURIO CORNER

Of corduroy and kings

It might be flattering to those who wear corduroy trousers or jackets if there were any basis for the belief that the word comes from *corde du roi*, 'the fabric of the king'. Sadly, this is no more than a prime example of unreliable popular etymology. *Cor* means 'corded', ribbed and *duroy* is an obsolete term for a form of coarse fabric.

crescendo

The word sounds rather like *crash* and this is probably why it is so often misused.

TEST YOURSELF

A. The brassy, braying sound of trombones rose to a magnificent crescendo at the end of the symphony.

B. On a moonless night, all other sounds in the woods were drowned out by the wind, rising to a crescendo as it howled through the trees.

C. The second movement of Beethoven's Seventh Symphony starts quietly then rises in a crescendo.

D. 'Abraham Lincoln's Gettysburg Address built towards a *crescendo*' (*Reader's Digest* word power article).

ANSWERS

A. *Crescendo* is used incorrectly.

B. Again, *crescendo* is misused.

C. *Crescendo* is used properly.

D. Despite the source, *crescendo* is misused.

Usage Tip

ℹ️ Sound rises *in* a crescendo, not *to* a crescendo. The word describes a process, not a result. Its Latin root *crescere* (to grow) means a gradual increase in the volume of sound – not a crashing finale. It is no more acceptable to describe something as rising *to a crescendo* than it would be to say it rises *to an increase*. Only bosses do that, at salary review time. If you are lucky.

CURIO CORNER

The curate and the egg

In a nineteenth-century *Punch* cartoon a nervous curate assures his bishop, who suggests that the poor man may have been served with a bad egg: 'Oh no, my Lord. Parts of it are excellent!' If only parts of an egg are bad, then the entire egg is spoiled. That is the point of the joke – a point that the cartoonist may have made in vain, for if an action or an idea is described as being 'a bit of a curate's egg', this is often taken, wrongly, to mean that while it may be unappealing in some ways it remains attractive in others.

d d d d D d d d d

---

dangling clause *See* **backing into sentences**

data

This word is plural and should not be used as if it were singular. The correct singular, *datum,* is not in common use because it sounds stiff. It is a word of Latin origin that has not yet been comfortably integrated into the English language. Even so, phrases such as *the assembled data shows* are to be avoided because they treat *data* as if it were singular. If you have found and are citing just a single piece of information, and *datum* sounds too formal, it is worth considering such words as *fact, research, evidence* or *information*. See also **agenda.**

deceptively

An estate agent who describes a kitchen as being *deceptively* large is presumably trying to persuade prospective buyers that the kitchen is bigger than it appears at first glance. But that is not what the words say. If a room is *deceptively* large, it looks more spacious than it is in fact. Similarly, one that is *deceptively* small – although no estate agent is likely to use such a term – is bigger than it may appear on first sight. The word *deceptively* is deceptive itself when it is used unthinkingly. Try *surprisingly* instead.

decimate

The Ancient Romans had a sharp way of dealing with a legion that mutinied or showed cowardice. One soldier in every ten was selected to be beaten or stoned to death by his comrades. Not surprisingly, this form of punishment did little for morale, and in time the Romans abandoned it. Sticklers for tradition in language if not in military discipline still insist that *decimate* should be used only when referring to a reduction by one tenth. Such diehards apart, most authorities now agree that *decimate* can be used to describe any event that causes a disastrous loss.

CURIO CORNER

Denim from Nîmes

The hard-wearing material from which jeans, and sometimes jackets and skirts, are made was originally called *serge de Nîmes*, because it was produced in the southern French city of Nîmes. When the fabric found a ready market in other countries it was a short step linguistically to abbreviate the name to *denim*. The spectacular expansion that has made denim a worldwide name came in 1853 when a 24-year-old German-American, Levi Strauss, set up a dry-goods business in San Francisco. The California gold rush was still going strong, and Levi Strauss built up stocks of canvas, which he thought would be in high demand for making tents and the covers for covered wagons. The prospectors, a tough breed of men, were more in need of tough clothing, so the young shopkeeper began making pants out of his plentiful supplies of canvas. He called them waist overalls, presumably because they came up to the waist.

It soon became clear to the prospectors that, tough as they were, stiff canvas was not a very comfortable material. More of a penance in a way, because it caused severe chafing. When they laid their complaints at the door of the young shopkeeper he remembered the softer, more pliant but still hard-wearing *serge de Nîmes* and switched to making the pants out of denim. The gold rush ended, but *denim*, also known as *Levis* and *blue jeans*, went on to conquer the world.

dependant/dependent

A *dependant* relies on somebody else, usually for upkeep. He or she is *dependent* on the other person. The two words are often confused, though the first is a noun and the second is an adjective.

TEST YOURSELF

A. My rich uncle left his dependants/dependents penniless. His entire fortune went to a cats' home.

B. Dependent/dependant on the weather we are planning an early start for Thursday's golf match.

C. My father, who was in his late 70s, decided to be independent/independant and to look after himself rather than be taken into a home.

D. There will be parades, bands and celebrations across the United States tomorrow because it is Independance/Independence Day, the Fourth of July.

ANSWERS

A. *Dependants*   **B.** *Dependent*   **C.** *Independent*   **D.** *Independence Day*

Usage Tips

ℹ️ *Depend*, the parent word of the noun dependant, comes from the Latin *de* (down) and *pendere* (to hang). *Dependent* is an adjective, and it is usually followed by *on*.

ℹ️ In American English, *dependent* and *independent* are accepted spellings for both the noun and the adjective.

deprecate/depreciate

Both are terms of disapproval, but there are important differences between them.

TEST YOURSELF

A. Many present-day comedians think it is amusing to depreciate/deprecate the Royal Family, although a generation or two ago this would have been unthinkable.

B. Harold is trying his best, so why is Elizabeth so keen on depreciating/deprecating his plans for re-designing the garden?

C. Be as self-depreciating/self-deprecating as you like, John. The credit for meeting this year's profit target belongs almost entirely to you.

D. During the hyper-inflation of 1923 Germany's currency depreciated/was depreated so rapidly that in Berlin the price of a ham sandwich increased by 10,000 Marks in a single day.

ANSWERS
A. *Deprecate*   **B**. *Deprecating*   **C**. *Self-deprecating*   **D**. *Depreciated*

Usage Tip

[i] Their Latin roots give a good clue to the differences between these two words. *Deprecate* comes from *de-* (away) + *precari* (to pray) and its original meaning was 'to ward off by prayer'. It carries the notion of disapproval, often with a hint of protest. *Depreciate* comes from *de-* + *petium* (price) and always carries the idea of a reduction in value, significance or price.

different from/to/than

Henry Fowler, the supreme and at times overbearing authority on the English usage of yesteryear, described the notion that *different* can be followed only by *from* as 'mere superstition'. It takes a bold writer to challenge Fowler, but many purists have chosen to ignore his advice.

TEST YOURSELF
A. Both the food and the standard of service in the hotel we chose this year are vastly different from/to/than what was on offer where we stayed last summer.

B. John's political opinions, formed from his wide reading and late night discussions with friends, are products of his age and background, which explains why they are different from/to/than his father's.

C. Annie carried herself differently from/to/than I had ever seen her before.

D. Let's hope that things turn out differently this year from/to/than they did the last time our team was chasing promotion.

E. The driver helped us to unload our luggage from his taxi without being asked – vastly different treatment from/to/than anything we had been led to expect.

F. Denise's tennis game has much improved since she started using a different backhand from/to/than the one she relied on last season.

G. I have always taken a different view of Michael's prospects from/to/than you.

ANSWERS

A. Both *different from* and *different to* are correct in British English. Americans would prefer *different than*.

B. *Different from. Different to* is also acceptable to a British ear, and *different than* to an American.

C. *Differently than.*

D. *Differently than.* If *from* is preferred, it should be followed by *how* or *the way.*

E. Traditionalists prefer *different from* or *to*, but d*ifferent than,* the preferred choice in America, is acceptable in everyday speech.

F. *Different from,* with *different to* as runner-up and *different than* as a first choice for Americans.

G. *Different than.*

Usage Tips

ℹ️ The British prejudice against *different than* is not always easy to justify, but *different from* is supported by tradition and by the fact that *from* emphasises the separation between two things that are being compared. If in doubt, use *from*.

ℹ️ *Different than*, the preferred usage in America, is also acceptable in Britain if, as in Sentence **G**, it is followed by a noun or a pronoun and results in a more elegant sentence than *different from*. Sentence **G**, for example, would have to be rewritten to justify *from,* and this could make it clumsy: *I have always taken a different view of Michael's prospects from the view you always take.*

ℹ️ If the word *from* already appears in the sentence, as in Sentences **B** and **E**, *different to* avoids repetition. This useful British alternative is rarely used by American speakers.

ℹ️ *Differently than* is preferable, with *differently to* as the runner-up, when followed by a clause, as in Sentences **C** and **D**.

CURIO CORNER

The devil's advocate

It can be irksome if, when you are putting forward a plan or sketching out an idea, somebody interrupts with the words: 'If I might play devil's advocate for a moment...' At best it means you are going to hear arguments that will put your infant proposals to a premature test. And all too often the interrupter has no firm belief in what he or she is saying, and is playing devil's advocate only to test how strongly you believe in your idea. The best response is to say something along the lines of: 'I know my plan is not perfect, but it's the best I have at the moment. How would you improve it, or do you have a different idea to put forward?'

The concept of a devil's advocate originated in the Roman Catholic process of beatification – that is, declaring that person to be blessed or on the path to full sainthood. The task of the advocate was to listen to a recital of holy deeds, miracles and other reasons why blessedness or sainthood should be conferred, then put the case against. Only then was it possible for a judgement to be reached.

discomfit/discomfort

These near lookalikes and close soundalikes have only a slight overlap in their meanings.

TEST YOURSELF

A. A good way to discomfort/discomfit a rich man who boasts about his wealth is to ask for a full and honest account of how he made his first million.

B. The actress tried to pass herself off as being in her twenties but, to her great discomfort/discomfiture, a gossip columnist revealed that she was in her forties.

C. For most Westerners, squatting on the heels can soon bring on a feeling of discomfort/discomfiture.

D. Napoleon was discomfited/discomforted, to say the least, when Blucher, at the head of more than 60,000 Prussians, arrived unexpectedly on the field of Waterloo.

E. The new shoes I bought caused real discomfort/discomfiture the first few times I wore them.

F. Imagine my discomfort/discomfiture when, as I bowed low, I heard the seam of my trousers rip apart.

G. In their long and bitter years of rivalry, Disraeli, with his scintillating wit, was usually able to discomfit/discomfort Gladstone, though he did not always emerge as the winner.

ANSWERS

A. *Discomfit*   **B.** *Discomfiture*   **C.** *Discomfort*   **D.** *Discomfited*
E. *Discomfort*   **F.** *Discomfiture*   **G.** *Discomfit*

Usage Tips

[i] *Discomfort* describes a state of feeling uncomfortable in body or mind. Because the word can imply mental uneasiness, it is sometimes confused with *discomfit*.

[i] To *discomfit* originally meant 'to defeat in battle', and that idea is still faintly echoed in its present-day meaning of 'to foil, to cause embarrassment, to distress or perplex'.

discover

To say that Columbus *discovered* America is to follow a Western convention without thinking. What Europeans called the New World was discovered long before Columbus – by distant ancestors of the people living there when he arrived. Give or take a Viking or two, it is correct to say that Columbus was the first European to discover America.

discreet/discrete

Confusion can arise when words with different meanings share the same pronunciation. A person who is *discreet* is reserved, judicious, trustworthy – somebody who can always be relied on to keep a secret: *Arthur's reputation for being discreet meant that people would tell him their innermost secrets with complete confidence.* *Discrete* means 'made up of parts that are separate and distinct': *Sand dunes may look like an immoveable range of low hills, but they are made up of billions of discrete grains and so are liable to form new shapes when the wind blows.*

disinterested/uninterested

These two words have swapped their meanings in the past, and have at other times been regarded as interchangeable. Today it is generally agreed that there is a clear distinction between them, and one that is worth preserving.

TEST YOURSELF
A. A judge is expected to be disinterested in the cases that he tries.
B. Arthur found James's offer of an unsecured loan to be not disinteresting.
C. Jenny was excited when she viewed what might become their new home, but David seemed entirely disinterested.
D. It isn't that I'm uninterested in crossword puzzles – it's just that I haven't much spare time these days.
E. We both believe you to be entirely disinterested, so Peter and I will be happy for you to hold the stakes when we make our bet.

ANSWERS
A. Correct. A judge who was *uninterested* in the case before him would probably miss some salient points, and might even nod off to sleep.
B. Incorrect. Moreover, the *not dis-* construction can sound awkward. *Not without interest* sounds better.
C. Incorrect. The word should be *uninterested*.
D. Correct.
E. Correct.

Usage Tips

ℹ️ In standard English, *disinterested* means 'impartial', and is applied to anybody who may be involved in a decision but has nothing either to gain or to lose by its outcome. *Uninterested* means 'indifferent, unconcerned, bored' and is applied to those who cannot summon up any interest in the outcome.

ℹ️ The useful distinction between the two words was blurred in former centuries and is not universally observed today – especially in parts of Scotland.

dived/dove

It used to be simple. For Americans and Canadians the usual past tense of dive was *dove*, and for Brits it was *dived*. The American version is now widely used in Britain, and is acceptable in informal contexts. Avoid it, though, if you want to sound correct.

double negative

What is the secret of the double negative? Why has it resisted the efforts of generations of schoolteachers to kill it off? If little Johnny claims: 'I wasn't doing nothing, Miss,' then logic dictates that he must have been doing something? And yet…

TEST YOURSELF

A. 'It wouldn't surprise me if Mark Cavendish doesn't pull out of the Tour de France' (BBC sports commentator).

B. This so-called master-plan of yours is bound to fail and I don't want no part of it.

C. I cannot believe that your proposal will not fail to find a backer.

D. 'I can't get no satisfaction' (Rolling Stones song).

E. 'I have one heart, one bosom and one truth/And that no woman has; nor never none/Shall be mistress be of it, save I alone' (William Shakespeare, *Twelfth Night*).

ANSWERS

A. The intention is clear enough. What the commentator means is that he would not be surprised if Mark Cavendish *did* pull out of the race. What he says is the opposite of this.

B. An inelegant and confusing double negative. The sentence should read: '...I don't want *any* part of it'.

C. There are so many negatives here that deciphering the meaning has become a Chinese puzzle. The solution is to cut out the negatives and keep things simple: *I believe that your proposal will fail to find a backer.*

D. It's a song, and one of their best, so why quibble about the grammar?

E. And who dares to correct Shakespeare?

Usage Tips

[i] In logic, two negatives cancel each other out, making a positive. So a schoolboy who insists he wasn't doing nothing is in fact admitting that he was doing something. However, schoolchildren are not bound by oath to follow the rules of logic.

[i] The double negative can call on Shakespeare as a defence witness too. See Sentence **E**.

[i] The double negative is a weed so vigorous that for centuries it has resisted all attempts to eradicate it. Nevertheless, this way of adding emphasis to a denial is best shunned by everyone who is not trying to reproduce the speech mannerisms of the uneducated, or who is neither a pop megastar nor William Shakespeare.

due to/owing to

In everyday language, these two phrases are interchangeable. Sticklers for the rules insist that there are real and important differences between them.

TEST YOURSELF

A. The 8.45 train has been delayed, due to/owing to leaves on the line.

B. Due to/owing to a heavy cold, Frank took a couple of days off work.

C. The firm went bankrupt, due to/owing to late payments and bad debts.

D. Due to/owing to a steep fall in the value of the £, fewer people are taking holidays abroad this year.

E. Jason's exclusion from the classroom, due to/owing to his long history of bad behaviour, lasted until the end of term.

F. The ending of the affair was mainly due to/owing to Charles's habit of eating his peas off a knife.

ANSWERS

A. *Owing to.*

B. *Owing to.*

C. Both terms are acceptable.

D. *Owing to.*

E. Both terms are acceptable.

F. Both terms are acceptable.

Usage Tips

ℹ️ Be wary of *due to*, especially at the start of a sentence. While it can almost always be replaced by *owing to,* grammarians have ruled that the reverse replacement is not always acceptable. The way they put it is that while *due to* and *owing to* can both function as adjectival phrases, *owing to* can also be used as a prepositional phrase, whereas *due to* cannot. This is not very helpful if you have to go to the reference books to check the meanings of *adjectival phrase* and *prepositional phrase*.

ℹ️ Fortunately, there is an easy way to follow the rule. Choose *owing to* when those two words can be replaced by *because of,* and use *due to* only when they can be replaced by *caused by,* without making the sentence sound odd.

ℹ️ Some modern authorities point out that there is no logic behind this rule and see no reason why *due to* should not be used as freely as *owing to*. They may win the argument some day, but until they do it is worth remembering the distinction between the two phrases.

CURIO CORNER

The clever dunce

The Scottish theologian and philosopher Duns Scotus (1266–1308) was one of the most admired scholars in mediaeval Europe. His teachings at Oxford, Paris and Cologne earned him the unofficial title of the 'Subtle Doctor'. Unfortunately for his later reputation they also brought him into conflict with the theologist known as the Angelic Doctor – Thomas Aquinas (1225–1274), who became one of the principal saints of the Roman Catholic Church. Scotus taught that faith depended on God's will, whereas Aquinas believed the existence of God could be proved by reason. The teachings of Scotus were discredited. During the Renaissance, a turmoil of ideas about art, scholarship, science and philosophy that began in the early 14th century, they were buried. By a cruel irony to be a dunce, or follower of the scholarly Duns Scotus, came to take on the meaning it has today: slow-witted, backward at learning and intellectually negligible.

E e e e E e e e e

each other/one another

The general rule is that *each other* should be used when two items are involved and *one another* when there are more than two. Like many linguistic rules, it can sometimes be broken with advantage. John Keats may have committed a historical howler when he implied that stout Cortez, rather than Vasco Nunez de Balboa, was the first Spanish *conquistador* to set eyes on the Pacific, but nobody is going to quarrel with him for ending his poem with:

> ... *and all his men*
> *Look'd at each other with a wild surmise –*
> *Silent, upon a peak in Darien.*

And even a purist is unlikely to object to being told: 'We love one another.'

effect *See* affect

effete

Whatever it may sound like, *effete* does not mean 'effeminate'. It means 'exhausted, listless, drained of energy'. This is easy to remember if you think of the word's derivation – from the Latin *ex*- (out) plus *fetus* (offspring), said of a woman who has been exhausted by years of child-bearing.

either

According to the rule, *either* should be used only when the choice lies between no more than two possibilities. But there are times when the rule can be broken. Another problem presented by *either* is that although it is a singular word it often sounds more natural when treated as if it were plural. *Either are* often manages to oust the more correct but less fluent-sounding *either is*.

TEST YOURSELF

A. They both queued for hours to get tickets for the concert, so it isn't remotely possible that either Sally or Jane intend to be anywhere else tonight.

B. I have never encountered such generous treatment before – either from close friends, casual acquaintances or even members of my own family.

C. Either the Bulgarians, with their young stars, or the Russians, with their new training techniques, stand a good chance of collecting a fistful of medals in the gymnastic events.

D. The football player with the best chance of being remembered as the greatest of all time is likely to be either Pele, George Best, Maradona or Messi.

E. 'On either side the river lie/Long fields of barley and of rye' (Lord Tennyson, *The Lady of Shallot*).

F. Either the Jones family or their landlord are going to have to foot the bill for repairing the roof.

G. You either pay back every penny of your expenses claim or I will report the matter to head office.

ANSWERS

A. Incorrect. It should be *either Sally or Jane intends*.

B. Although the 'two only' rule is broken, this sentence is acceptable in everyday speech. To make it grammatically correct, without calling for a rewrite, the word *either* could be dropped.

C. *Stand* is correct.

D. Again the rule is broken, but in a way that is acceptable in an informal context. To be beyond reproach, delete *either*.

E. Tennyson's use of *either* might be criticised by those who rank pedantry higher than poetry. He should have written *on both sides*, they could say. But what is good enough for a Poet Laureate is surely good enough for the rest of us.

F. There is no satisfactory way of deciding between *are* and *is* in this sentence. The best solution would be to rewrite it, along the lines of: *Either the Jones family or their landlord will have to foot the bill for repairing the roof.*

G. This '*either ... or*' sentence is not properly balanced. See **Usage Tips**.

Usage Tips

[i] Only a diehard pedant would object to the way the 'two only' rule is ignored in Sentences **B** and **D**. Even so it is a good idea to keep to this rule whenever possible.

[i] *Either* calls for a singular verb if both of the possible choices are singular (Sentence **A**) and a plural verb if they are plural (Sentence **C**). If one possibility is singular and the other is plural (Sentence **F**) the convention is to make the verb agree with the subject that is nearest to it. If the sentence still sounds awkward, reword it.

[i] The placing of *either...or* in a sentence calls for some care. The clause introduced by *either* should always be balanced in its construction by the clause introduced by *or*. Sentence **G**, for example, should read: *Either you pay back every penny of your expenses claim or I will report the matter to head office.*

[i] *You say eether, I say eyether* – so goes the song. It comes to the conclusion that both pronunciations are acceptable, as indeed they are. *Eyether* happens to be more favoured in Britain and eether in America, but neither pronunciation is wrong in either version of the language. See also **neither**.

electrical terms

A few pointers for those whose science may be a little rusty:

◆ *amp:* measures the rate of flow of an electrical current. Short for ampère and named after the French physicist Andre Marie Ampère (1775–1836).

◆ *joule*: a unit of energy, equal to the amount of one amp passed through a resistance of one ohm for one second. Named after the British physicist James Prescott Joule (1818–89).

◆ *ohm*: a measure of electrical resistance. Named after the German physicist Georg Simon Ohm (1789–1854).

◆ *volt*: a unit of electrical force. One volt is sufficient to send one amp through a resistance of one ohm. Named after the Italian physicist Count Alessandro Volta (1745–1827).

◆ *watt*: a unit of electrical power. Named after the Scottish engineer James Watt (1736–1819).

emigrant/immigrant

These two words are not likely to be confused so long as you think of their origins. The Latin prefix *ex-* means 'out of', as in *exit*, while the prefix *in-*, from which the *imm* in *immigrant* derives, means 'into'. A family that leaves Britain to make a new life in another country are *emigrants* from the land of their birth and, until they have settled in, *immigrants* in their new country. Migration is not always permanent: *migrant workers* usually intend to return to their home country and *migrant birds* fly thousands of miles back and forth as part of the seasonal patterns of their lives.

emulate

Does it mean 'to imitate', 'to strive to equal' or 'to surpass'? Emulate can mean any of these, and the context should make it clear which meaning is intended.

endemic/epidemic/pandemic

All three words have Greek roots, and the one they have in common is *demos* (the people), which gives us, among other words, democracy. But can you sort out *en-* from *epi-* and *pan-* ?

TEST YOURSELF

A. Almost 20 million people died in the 'flu epidemic/endemic/pandemic that followed the First World War – a heavier toll than that taken by the war itself.

B. Bubonic Plague, spread by rat fleas and known in the Middle Ages as the Black Death, was for centuries endemic/epidemic/pandemic in the Far East.

C. An endemic/epidemic/pandemic of destruction swept through Lancashire in 1825, when starving handloom weavers turned against the machines that had put them out of work.

ANSWERS
A. *Pandemic*   **B**. *Endemic*   **C**. *Epidemic*

Usage Tips

[i] *En-* means 'in', as in envelope, so an *endemic* disease is one that is inherent in a particular group of people or in a particular region.

[i] *Epi-* means 'among' or 'over', so an *epidemic* disease is one that spreads rapidly among the people living in a stated area.

[i] *Pan-* means 'all', so a *pandemic* disease is one that has spread across or is a serious threat to people in a number of countries or regions.

[i] All three words can be applied by extension to outbreaks that are not connected with disease – an *epidemic* of road rage, for example.

enervate

It is tempting to believe that *enervate* means the same as *energise*. In fact, it means the opposite: 'to drain of energy'. Its roots are the Latin words: *ex- (to remove)* plus *nervus* (nerve or sinew), so its literal meaning is *'to remove the sinews'*.

enjoy

Those who use this word on its own risk annoying careful speakers. *Enjoy* is a transitive verb, which means it takes a direct object, so mention must always be made of whatever is meant to be enjoyed. You *enjoy* a meal or a party, a concert, a good argument and so forth. The stand-alone command *Enjoy!* is an American import which so far has not been accepted in Britain as standard English.

enormity

What was once a clear distinction between *enormity* and *enormousness* is beginning to show signs of breaking down. Careful speakers, however, hold on to the difference between them.

TEST YOURSELF

A. The enormity of the task did not dawn on John until he saw what a mountain of rubbish would have to be carted away before the builders could even make a start on the new house.

B. In less enlightened days, people used to buy tickets to sneak a look at bearded ladies, two-headed goats and suchlike enormities on display in freak shows.

C. The enormity of the tsunami that hit the coast of Japan in 2011 was almost beyond belief.

D. The most impressive aspect of the Great Pyramid, for those viewing it for the first time, is its sheer enormity.

E. 'For many years after the war, the Soviet régime suppressed admission or discussion of the enormity of the sacrifice imposed by its failure to feed Leningrad's inhabitants' (*The Sunday Times*, book review).

ANSWERS

A. Incorrect. *Enormousness* would be appropriate, though it would sound ungainly. Say something like *enormous size* or *vastness* instead.

B. *Enormities* is correct.

C. Incorrect. Say *overwhelming height, enormous height* or *towering size*.

D. Incorrect. Say *sheer enormousness*.

E. Incorrect. Try *immensity of the sacrifice* or *enormous sacrifice*.

Usage Tips

[i] *Enormity* does not mean 'huge in size or number'. It should be applied only to deeds or thoughts that are outrageous, monstrous, wicked or in some other way beyond the pale.

[i] Though rather awkward and ungainly, *enormousness* is the correct word for something that is exceptionally large. Because it sounds clumsy, the word is often avoided, and this may well explain why the useful distinction between *enormity* and *enormousness* has become blurred.

[i] Handy alternatives to *enormousness* are *vastness* and *immensity*.

enquiry/inquiry

In British English an *enquiry* is a question about a matter of private interest, whereas an *inquiry* is an investigation into a question of public interest. A private individual might make an *enquiry* about how to get tickets for a Wimbledon Final, but a government will set up an *inquiry* into the spread of foot-and-mouth disease. The distinction between the verb forms, *enquire* and *inquire,* is maintained rather less doggedly than that between the noun forms *enquiry* and *inquiry*. In America, *inquire* and *inquiry* have the field almost entirely to themselves.

CURIO CORNER

How can an exception prove a rule?

Think about it for a moment and it will become clear that the phrase *the exception proves the rule* does not make sense. How can a rule-breaking exception demonstrate that the rule is valid and true? But *proof* has another meaning. It can also describe the process of determining quality or purity by way of a scientific test. An alcoholic drink, for instance, may be described as 80% proof spirit. It is only in this sense of putting the rule to a test that the saying makes any sort of sense.

envelope

Pronounced **en**-velope. Some people risk sounding pretentious by pronouncing this word with more than due deference to its French origin: **on**-velope or even **ong**-velope.

Eskimo

The idea has got abroad that *Eskimo* is an insulting term because it means 'eater of raw flesh' and that we should say *Inuit* instead. Mmm... perhaps. Every large population group has the right to be known by the name it prefers, and most of the indigenous inhabitants of the Arctic region regard themselves as being *Inuit*. Most, but not all. Even so, unless you have a detailed knowledge of Arctic languages and cultures it is on balance safer to use *Inuit* and avoid *Eskimo*.

Esq

Whether you use this abbreviation or *Mr* when writing an address is largely a matter of age – both yours and the recipient's. It is a courtesy title, short for *Esquire*, and it used to imply that the recipient, though not entitled to be addressed by some such title as *Lord, Sir, Professor, Dr* or *The Rev.* was, still, by birth or behaviour, a gentleman. The modern tendency is to use plain *Mr*, but *Esq.* is still favoured by those who like to be reminded of a more polite era.

CURIO CORNER

An eye for an eye

The phrase *an eye for an eye, a tooth for a tooth*, first set down in the code of Hammurabi, king of Babylon 1792–1750 BC, is generally taken as giving legal sanction to vengeance as an approved form of justice. A more likely interpretation is that Hammurabi was more concerned with setting limits to revenge than with condoning harsh punishments, and that the phrase means: *no more than an eye for an eye, no more than a tooth for a tooth.*

etc

Unless you are writing a business letter it can sound dismissive to round off a list with the abbreviated form of the Latin *et cetera* ('and the rest of them'). It is warmer to use English and write *and so on, and so forth* or *and suchlike*. A common, and sadly revealing, mistake with the spoken word is to pronounce it *ek-cetera*.

f f f F F F f f f

fabulous

Like a heavyweight boxer sent into the ring against a succession of flyweights, *fabulous* has in recent years been doing a job that is far below its capabilities. Inevitably, it has lost much of its power. In a revealing sign of weakness, the over-used *fabulous* has come to need the assistance of a crutch: the adverb *absolutely*. Careful speakers will use *fabulous* sparingly, and bear in mind its close connection with *fable*. The fairytale castles built for mad King Ludwig of Bavaria are *fabulous*. A new hat for Ascot is not, no matter how decorative.

> ### CURIO CORNER
>
> ### *Fans and fanatics*
>
> The Latin word *fanum* means 'temple' and in Ancient Rome anybody who was closely connected to a temple was a *fanaticus*. This word came to be applied to those whose zeal came so close to mania that they were believed to be possessed – either by gods or by demons. *Fanatic* came into the English language with its original meanings but late in the nineteenth century it entered the world of sport and added a new one, in the abbreviated form of *fan*. The parent word now conjures up dark associations. To be a *fan* is to be an enthusiast. To be a *fanatic* is to be a menace.

fantastic

Give your address to somebody who asks for it on the telephone and the response may well be: *Fantastic!* You know, and the caller knows, that such praise is too lavish for a mental feat that demands nothing more taxing than the ability to remember where you live. So why use the word? As with *fabulous,* the more *fantastic* is over-used, the more its meaning drains away. It would be going too far, perhaps, to deny the term to sports commentators, but outside their sphere it should be used sparingly.

farther/further

Which of these two you choose is largely a matter of which sounds better to your ear. In the nineteenth century a rule emerged that *farther* should be used for physical distance, and *further* for figurative distance. A passenger might ask: 'How much *farther* do we have to go before we get to your house?' A politician might say: 'It all depends on how much *further* you are prepared to push your argument.' Trying to preserve such a distinction today would look decidedly old-fashioned. In any case, *farther* seems to be going out of fashion – a development that has gone faster and *further* in Britain than in America.

ferment/foment

These two are easy to confuse because both can mean 'to stir up trouble'. But they have separate meanings too, arising from their separate origins.

TEST YOURSELF
A. It was plain to the prison governor that trouble had been fermenting/fomenting since the jail's most notorious inmate applied for a job in the library and was turned down.
B. Lenny was well known among dockers for his skill in fermenting/fomenting unrest.
C. King Leopold II treated the Belgian Congo as if it were his private money-making estate, and resentment among its oppressed inhabitants fomented/fermented for decades.

ANSWERS
A. *Fermenting* is the likelier choice, but *fomenting* would be

appropriate if the would-be librarian was turned down several months or even weeks before trouble erupted.

B. Either word is suitable, depending on whether Lenny's contribution to industrial relations lay in his skill at fostering an atmosphere of grumbling and dissatisfaction (fomenting) or in heightening resentment during an outbreak of unrest (*fermenting*).

C. *Fomented.*

Usage Tips

ℹ️ *Ferment* comes from the Latin *fermentum* (yeast). When yeast is added to dough it causes the seething, turbulence and bubbling known as fermentation.

ℹ️ The original meaning of *fomentation* was the application of a warm poultice to the skin. By extension, *to foment* has also come to mean 'to warm things up'. It stands close to *ferment* as a slower and usually less violent accomplice in the business of stirring up trouble.

fewer/less

The general rule is that *fewer* refers to items that can be counted, whereas *less* is used for quantities that are measured or estimated in other ways. There are, however, times when it is safe to ignore the rule.

TEST YOURSELF
A. A regular charge levelled against the National Health Service is that it needs a few more doctors and nurses on the wards and a few less managers telling them what to do.

B. Any athlete who has run the 1500 m in less than 3 min 40 sec has more than a good chance of winning the next race.

C. 'Less Than 10 Items' (notice at supermarket check-out).

D. I could do with losing some weight so I'm going to eat less butter and take less lumps of sugar in my tea.

E. With less than 24 hours to go before kick-off, the manager had still not decided who should play in goal.

ANSWERS

A. *Fewer managers* is correct if you insist on following the rule. But *a few fewer* sounds clumsy. This justifies saying *a few less managers* if the context is fairly informal. If not, try *not so many managers*.

B. Sport belongs to the informal side of life, and the informal *less than four minutes* is acceptable. *Fewer than four minutes*, though it keeps to the rule, sounds pedantic.

C. Such notices have been known to upset members of the old school, who point out that the word should be *fewer*. They cannot be faulted over their concern for the language, but perhaps they might turn a blind eye to a minor slip, and accept that the supermarket's message is both commendably short and perfectly clear.

D. Less butter is fine, but the rule dictates using fewer lumps of sugar, not less lumps.

E. The rule calls for *fewer* than 24 hours, but in this case *less* than is perfectly acceptable because it is a usage of long standing.

Usage Tips

ℹ️ When in doubt, follow the rule, using *fewer* for those things that can be counted and *less than* for those that cannot. But if this makes what you say sound clumsy, it is better to ignore the rule.

ℹ️ Although time, distance and money are made up of units that can clearly be counted, *less than* is perfectly acceptable in such usages as *less than four minutes, less than 10 miles* and *less than £20*. Idiom is more powerful than any rule.

factitious/fictitious

The difference in meaning between these two is worth knowing and preserving.

TEST YOURSELF

A. The teacher's pet, who was slightly built and rather timid, gave a fictitious/factitious account of how he had given the playground bully a black eye.

B. The MP gave a fictitious/factitious explanation of why he had put in expense claims for two second homes at the same time.

C. The stock market's dotcom bubble was bound to burst because so many share prices were based on forecasts so optimistic as to be fictitious/factitious.

ANSWERS

A. *Fictitious.*

B. *Factitious.*

C. Either word would be correct, depending on whether the share price forecasts were deliberately fraudulent *(fictitious)* or caused by over-enthusiastic but ill-founded optimism *(factitious)*.

Usage Tips

ℹ️ *Fictitious* means 'imaginary, unreal, untrue', and is closely linked to its parent word, *fiction*.

ℹ️ The similar-sounding *factitious* means 'artificial, contrived, misleading, produced for the sake of effect without strict regard for the truth'. It can come very close in meaning to *fictitious*, but it does not amount to outright lying.

CURIO CORNER

If something is flammable, how can it be inflammable too?

We have come to expect the Latin-based prefix *in-* to carry a negative charge. It can turn a *visible* human being into the *Invisible Man*, or make a performance that seems adequate to untrained ears sound inadequate in the opinion of a professional critic. But this prefix can be an intensifier as well as a negation. To avoid confusion the new word *flammable* was added to the language more than a century ago. It would have made things tidier if, at the same time, the older word had been evicted. But it wasn't – with the result that *flammable* and *inflammable* mean one and the same thing.

first/firstly

There used to be a prejudice against starting a list with *Firstly*. It was urged with some vehemence that the right sequence was *First ... secondly... thirdly ... fourthly ...* and so on. This 'rule' is taking longer to die than an overweight diva in an opera's last Act, but there was never any logic to it, and it can safely be ignored.

flaunt/flout

One of the most persistent errors in the English language is to confuse *flaunt* with *flout*.

TEST YOURSELF
A. If you've got it, flaunt/flout it!
B. There are still people who believe they are morally justified in flaunting/flouting the rules when they fill in their tax return.
C. It is not unheard of for golfers who dress as soberly as bank managers during the working week to flaunt/flout outrageously garish colours when they take to the course.

ANSWERS
A. *Flaunt.*
B. *Flouting.*
C. *Flaunt.*

Usage Tip
[i] To *flaunt* means 'to show off'. To *flout* means 'to disregard, scorn or treat with contempt'. How the two became confused is a mystery.

flotsam/jetsam/ligan

Anything of value found floating in the sea after a wreck is *flotsam*. Goods that are washed ashore or that sink after being thrown overboard are *jetsam*. Anything that goes down with the ship or is marked by a buoy to claim ownership is *ligan*. *Flotsam* and *jetsam* can be kept by the finder unless the owner can prove a legal claim to them.

Ligan, which for most of us is more likely to be encountered in a pub quiz than on the high seas, belongs to the owner, no matter who finds it.

flout *See* flaunt

foreign phrases

Apart from an occasional *Bon Voyage!* when a friend sets out on a long journey or a *Gesundheit!* when someone is sneezing, the seasoning of language with foreign words and phrases is no longer in fashion – if only because foreign words are far from certain these days to be understood. It may be tempting to drop a Latin phrase into your speech or writing but it can be a mistake to do so unless you are sure of your ground. A candidate for promotion ruled himself out when he told his rival: 'I don't care if the boss has agreed that you will be *primus inter pares*, so long as it's clear that we will both be absolutely equal.' And a spokesman in a dispute over who should be the head of a nationally known retail chain made himself sound ridiculous when he said, in a BBC interview: 'We are not objecting to Rose *per se*. We are objecting to Rose himself.' The moral is obvious.

for ever/forever

The two-word spelling conveys the notion of something that is eternal or everlasting: *We vowed to be friends for ever.* The one-word spelling is an emphatic way of saying 'constantly': *She was forever popping in and out of our house.* This useful distinction is in danger of being lost, with *forever* taking on both jobs. *Forever* appears to have entirely supplanted *for ever* in the USA and is well on the way to doing the same in Britain. But it's worth making the point that if it succeeds, the language will have lost a shade of meaning. Just as we still have a few red squirrels resisting the advance of their grey cousins, so we still have a few purists who insist on maintaining the distinction between *forever* and *for ever.*

former … latter

There is an unwritten understanding that a reader should not be expected to do the work of the writer. This means it is worth thinking twice before using the construction *the former…the latter.* This reminder of who did what can be useful at times but it becomes a nuisance if it forces the reader to go back and work out who or what is meant by *the former* and who or what by *the latter.* He or she is then at risk of losing your drift, and you are in danger of losing your reader. There are, of course, times when the construction is useful – as, for instance, in Thomas Love Peacock's:

> The mountain sheep are sweeter,
> But the valley sheep are fatter;
> We therefore deemed it meeter
> To carry off the latter.

(But deemed? Meeter? Latter? Clearly this was no run-of-the-mill sheep-stealer.)

fortuitous

This word does not mean 'fortunate' but is often used as if it did.

TEST YOURSELF
A. Sally and Margaret met fortunately/fortuitously after both decided, on the spur of the moment, to take a stroll in the park.

B. It was doubly fortunate/fortuitous that they bumped into each other because Margaret needed a babysitter and Sally was short of cash.

C. One of the arguments put forward to support the theory of Intelligent Design is that the human eye, with all its complexities, could not be simply the end product of a vast number of fortunate/fortuitous circumstances.

ANSWERS

A. *Fortuitously.*

B. *Fortunate.*

C. Either word could be appropriate, depending on whether the piling up of circumstances should be regarded as due to luck *(fortunate)* or to pure chance *(fortuitous)*.

Usage Tips

ℹ️ *Fortuitous* means 'by chance, unplanned, unanticipated, happening by accident'.

ℹ️ Because it is possible for something to happen as the result of a lucky accident, there is an increasing tendency to fall into the error of using *fortuitous* as if it meant the same as *fortunate*.

free (for free)

Strictly speaking, a packet of biscuits offered as an inducement to buy the first packet is not *for free*. It is either *free* or yours *for nothing*. However, it is pointless to condemn an expression that has won a firm foothold in the high street, in television advertising, and in the press. *For free* is clearly here to stay, although it is deplored by careful users of the language. They will probably hold to this view at least until the publishers of Monopoly add *for* to the cards that carry the message 'Get out of Jail free'.

frequent

When the word is used as an adjective, meaning 'often' the accent is placed on the first syllable: ***fre****quent*. When it is used as a verb, meaning 'habitually visiting a particular place or in the company of a particular person' the accent is on the second syllable: *frequent* and *frequenting*. Stressing the verb on the first syllable, in the same way as the noun, is not standard English. In America, however, this pronunciation is encountered so often that it may not be far from becoming standard.

fulsome

It is widely believed that *fulsome* is simply an emphatic way of saying *full*. Its true meaning is 'lavish, excessive, over-abundant'. *Fulsome praise* can be insincere to the point of becoming cloying. A *fulsome* apology can be so humble and self-deprecating that it might have come out of the mouth of Uriah Heep.

furore/furor

Should *furore* be pronounced Italian style, with three syllables, or are two enough? Three syllables ousted two in Britain in the nineteenth century, possibly as a result of Italian immigration. America has had its share of Italian immigrants, too, but the older two-syllable pronunciation and spelling have resisted change there.

further *See* farther

g g g ⁛ G g g g g

---

gaol *See* **jail**

garage

The *Oxford English Dictionary* allows two possible pronunciations, both placing the accent on the first syllable. Its first choice has the second syllable rhyming with the French pronunciation of dressage and its second choice rhymes it with porridge. The American pronunciation, which is gaining a foothold in Britain but has yet to earn widespread approval, places the accent on the second syllable.

CURIO CORNER

Gerrymandering the boundaries

Harvard graduate Elbridge Gerry, governor of Massachusetts from 1810 to 1812, was inclined to be over-zealous when elections came round. He shamelessly arranged for district boundaries to be redrawn, so that seats in the Senate would be more likely to be won by his own party, the Democratic Republicans. One district became so twisted and convoluted that critics said it took the shape, on a map, of a salamander. From that time onwards, fiddling electoral boundaries for the sake of electoral advantage has been labelled gerrymandering.

---

gerund

Purists will fight to the last ditch for the survival of the gerund, a noun that began life as a verb. They prefer, for instance, 'I object to *his* taking that attitude' to 'I object to *him* taking that attitude'. There is no question that, to ears unschooled in Latin, the gerund sounds pedantic, even pretentious. Nevertheless, it is not advisable to banish it entirely, especially when using formal English. The reward for *your* (not *you*) using it is that those who care for the language will listen more attentively to what you have to say.

gobsmacked

A vulgarism that appears to be confined to British English. It is better to say *astounded, flabbergasted* or *astonished*.

good

Increasingly, the question 'How are you?' is answered with: 'I'm good!' This development is favoured by youngsters but deplored by traditionalists, who regard it as an intrusive Americanism. In time it may be absorbed into British English, but that time has not yet arrived.

gourmand/gourmet

The first is a glutton, who shovels down food with little regard for its quality. The second is a connoisseur who delights in choosing the finest of foods. The two rarely meet in the same person.

graffiti

More than one message sprayed on a wall and you are looking at *graffiti*. If there is only one message or image, it is a *graffito*.

Greek/Grecian

The people are *Greek* and so is the language. The art, architecture and literature of ancient Greece used to be described as *Grecian,* but nowadays *Greek* is often used when referring to cultural matters, too. If Keats were writing his *Ode on a Grecian urn* today he might well have addressed it to a *Greek vase*.

grow

A market gardener can grow potatoes, a man can grow a beard, a child can grow taller. But is *grow* the right word when referring to increasing profits and market share? This usage has established a firm place in the business world and there, perhaps, is where it should be left. And what, after all, was wrong with *expanding* a business or *increasing* its profits?

h h h H h ɧ h h

hails from

As a way of saying 'comes from', *hails from* is old fashioned, almost archaic. Can a man living in Wales be described as hailing from New Zealand? Not unless he has a superhumanly powerful set of lungs.

hanged/hung

Pictures and decorative plates are *hung* on the wall, and grouse are *hung* in preparation for the table. When unpopular dictators fall they are likely to be *hanged* in effigy, and highwaymen, popular or unpopular, were once *hanged* in reality. This useful distinction between the word applicable to human beings and that applied to inanimate objects is worth preserving. It has come under threat recently, with *hung* beginning to edge out *hanged* whatever the context. Careful writers and speakers resist this development.

harass

Until 30 years or so ago, there was only one acceptable pronunciation: *harass*, with the stress on the first syllable. Since then, in line with a tendency in the language for the stress to shuffle to the right, and perhaps under the influence of television sitcoms, *harass* has also become acceptable – to all but those who have a high regard for traditional usage.

he/she/they

The personal pronouns *they, them, their, theirs, your* and *yours* can refer to either gender, but *he, him, his* and *she, her, hers* are gender-specific, and this can sometimes cause a problem. See also **sexist language**.

TEST YOURSELF

A. If a customer makes a complaint about the service they receive in this shop, then she is entitled to a civil answer.

B. Whoever wins the race for promotion will have a tough job on his hands.

C. When you find out who left their glasses behind the sofa, give them back to him or her with my compliments.

D. If somebody has been electrocuted in the house, turn off the electricity at the mains before you touch him or her.

E. Anybody who wins the Lottery will soon find he or she has plenty of friends who will be more than happy to help him or her to find ways of spending the money.

F. In the old days, if a child misbehaved in class the teacher would stand them in a corner and give him or her time to reflect.

G. 'The new leader will then be given about 12 months to establish themselves' (Andrew Porter, in the *Daily Telegraph*).

ANSWERS

A. Using *she* makes the assumption that complaints will be made by a woman, when they might equally well come from a man. Substitute either *that person* or *he or she* and the sentence sounds a little clumsy. The best solution would be to rewrite along the lines: *Any customer who complains … is entitled to a civil answer.*

B. The unwarranted assumption here is that only men are in line for promotion. Rewrite along the lines: *Whoever gets promoted will be taking on a tough job.*

C. The glasses belonged to one person, so the colloquially acceptable 'left *their* glasses' is grammatically incorrect. Say *'these glasses'* instead. 'Give them back *to him or her'* is grammatically correct but it makes for an awkward-sounding sentence. In any case it is unnecessary: *to him or her* can be deleted without any loss to the meaning.

D. Again, there is nothing ungrammatical about *him or her*. But this phrase can be overused. To avoid this, say *the victim*.

E. *He or she* is fine, but using *him or her* in the same sentence sounds clumsy. Say instead: *to help in finding ways of spending the money.*

F. Only in informal speech is it allowable to sidestep the *him or her* problem by switching from the singular (*child*) to the plural (*them*). Say instead *the trouble maker*. The use of *him or her* in the second half of Sentence **F** is correct, but be on guard against its overuse.

G. The new leader appears to have cloned himself or herself, and miraculously to have become become plural. Say instead *to become established*.

Usage Tips

[i] There are two ways to avoid sounding sexist when using singular personal pronouns. One is to spell out *he or she, him or her* and *his or hers*. This can make a sentence sound clumsy and will soon become monotonous if it is overdone. The other is to recast the sentence:

[i] Just about the worst thing you can do when faced with the *he or she* problem is to get into a tangle by switching from singular to plural, as in Sentences **F** and **G**.

hiccup/hiccough

Either spelling is acceptable, but in line with a trend towards keeping life simple, hiccup is becoming the first choice.

hippopotamus

The plural is *hippopotamuses,* not *hippopotami*.

historic/historical

In 1215, when King John set his seal to Magna Carta at Runnymede it was both a *historic* occasion and a *historical* one. But generally the two words are not so readily interchangeable.

TEST YOURSELF

A. Sir Walter Scott could fairly be described as the father of the historic/ historical novel.

B. The Taff Vale judgement of 1901 is regarded as a historic/historical decision because the reaction it provoked helped to create Britain's Labour Party.

C. It was a truly historic/historical meeting when the path of the wealthy motor car enthusiast Charles Stewart Rolls crossed with that of the engineer Frederick Henry Royce.

D. The day you offered to cook the Christmas dinner and burned the turkey has gone down as a historic/historical moment in the annals of our family.

ANSWERS

A. *Historical*   **B.** *Historic*   **C.** *Historic*   **D.** *Historic* (jocular)

Usage Tips

ℹ️ *Historic* is the word to reach for when you refer to an event or decision so important that it made history. It can also be used jokingly to lend an aura of mock importance to minor events. *Historical* is the right choice to describe something that happened in the past or that refers to the study of history.

ℹ️ Both *a* historic/historical and *an* historic/historical are acceptable pronunciations. Use *a* if the *h* is pronounced, and *an* if you prefer the *h* to be silent.

hoard/horde

Surprising though it may be, these two sound-alikes are sometimes confused in what are usually regarded as being serious newspapers. A *hoard* is a hidden store of food or treasure. Squirrels *hoard* nuts, to be eaten in times of scarcity. Pirates *hoard* jewellery and gold coins and bury them in the sand, to be squabbled over later. Sensible householders *hoard* food in cupboards and larders, as a form of insurance against prices rising too high or the supermarkets running out of stock. The Anglo-Saxons knew all about hard times, for *hoard* was one of their contributions to the language.

A *horde* is a swarm of people, animals or insects. *The Golden Horde*, for instance, was a Mongol army that swept on horseback across much of eastern Europe and a large chunk of Siberia in the 13th century. The word comes from the Turkish *ordu,* a camp, and *Urdu,* the language of the camp, is the Hindustani language bearing the same name.

hoi polloi

This expression, signifying 'the masses' or 'the common people', comes from the Greek words *hoi,* meaning 'the' and *polloi,* meaning 'many'. It is therefore a mistake to refer to *the hoi polloi,* since this is one *the* too many.

honestly, to be honest

For the most part, such words and phrases are fairly harmless. They add nothing to the meaning of a statement, but give people time to collect their thoughts. In this way they perform much the same function as the *umms* and *errs* of the spoken word. Be careful, though, not to draw attention too frequently to your honesty. It could give rise to a suspicion that you are protesting too much.

hopefully

An acid test of your attitude towards changes in the language is whether or not you approve of the 'new' way of using *hopefully.* Do you find it acceptable only when it means *with hope in your heart,* or *in a hopeful manner?* Did Robert Louis Stevenson settle the question beyond doubt when he wrote: 'To travel hopefully is a better thing than to arrive'? Or do you believe that *hopefully* can also bear the meaning *it is to be hoped that* – as in such statements as: '*Hopefully,* we will arrive in good time for lunch'? Older people and those who object to the Americanisation of the language (often one and the same group) tend to line up with Stevenson. Those on the other side of the argument could point out that few object to such statements as: '*Mercifully,* the singing was not too loud' or 'The restaurant was pricier than I expected, but *thankfully* I had enough money left to pay the bill', So why shun the extended use of *hopefully?* The best solution, perhaps, is to accept that the new usage is now well established but to bear in mind that it will almost certainly continue to offend traditionalists for a while yet.

horde *See* **hoard**

hyper/hypo

These prefixes have opposite meanings, but may sometimes be confused. To avoid going wrong, think of a *hyper*active child creating havoc in the classroom and a worried teacher asking a *hypo*thetical question about the possibility of transferring that child to another school. *Hyper* means 'over, above, to an excessive degree' – as in hypertension (high blood pressure), hypersensitive and hypercritical. *Hypo* means' under, below, beneath' – as in hypotension (abnormally low blood pressure), hypodermic needle (used for injections beneath the skin) and hypothesis (an assertion or idea that may possibly be true but has not yet been proven).

CURIO CORNER

Is good acting a form of hypocrisy?

Sincerity is one of the most prized attributes of any actor, so it seems more than a trifle unfair that the Ancient Greek word for enthralling an audience in the theatre was *hupokrisis,* the origin of our word *hypocrite.* The link probably arose because the greater the actor the more successful he or she is at pretending to be somebody else.

ı̃ ı ı ı̈ I ı ı ı i

I/me *See* **between you and I**

if *See* **subjunctive mood**

if/whether/whether or not

The widespread use of *if*, rather than *whether* or *whether or not* can occasionally cause problems.

TEST YOURSELF
A. John didn't know if/whether he should laugh or cry when the police told him they had found his stolen car, but it was so badly damaged that it was a write-off.
B. I find this sauce as tangy as any I have tasted, if/whether or not a little past its sell-by date.
C. I really need to know if/whether you are likely to be at home next Thursday.

D. The rising star's game was improving at such a rate that it became a question not so much of if/whether he would win a grand slam title but of how soon this was going happen.

E. If/whether or not you carry on making that infernal row I'm going to give your drum kit away to the nearest charity shop.

F. If it was/were left entirely to me I would overlook what seems to be an entirely innocent mistake.

ANSWERS

A. *Whether.*

B. *Whether or not.* Choosing *if* makes the sentence ambiguous. Does it mean *although* or is the speaker saying that the sauce tastes tangy *only* if it is a little past its sell-by date?

C. *Whether.*

D. *Whether.*

E. Either *if* or *whether or not* is suitable, depending on what the speaker intends to say. *If* implies that the drum kit will be given away unless the row stops. *Whether or not* means that whatever happens the drums are destined to go to the charity shop.

F. *If it was* will pass muster for informal speech and writing, but the grammatically correct wording is *if it were*.

Usage Tips

ⓘ *If* is appropriate when a condition is laid down: *If you want to claim the prize you will need to produce your ticket*. Both *whether* and *whether or not* are used when a choice is available: *I can't remember whether/whether or not you like spinach*.

ⓘ Sometimes, as in Sentence **B**, *if* can lead to ambiguity.

illusion *See* allusion

immigrant *See* emigrant

impact

Consider this sentence: *Charles Darwin's theory of evolution impacted on the scientific world in a way that radically changed our thinking.* Few people would object to the idea expressed, but purists would deplore the manner of expressing it. In North America, *impact* has been accepted as a verb for almost a century, but in Britain there are many who feel uncomfortable with this usage. They prefer *influenced, affected, changed* or *had an effect on*. Until *impact* as a verb has become better established it is perhaps better to avoid using it as one in the UK.

implement

As a noun, *implement* is no worse than a somewhat pretentious way of referring to a tool. As a verb, it invites criticism because it is over-used. Let politicians or industrialists wanting to sound important talk of *implementing* their plans and policies, say the purists; but, for the rest of us, what is wrong with *carry out, perform, accomplish* or *put into effect*?

imply/infer

When somebody asks, usually in an arch tone of voice: 'Are you *inferring*...?' there is a high probability that what is meant is: 'Are you *implying*...?' The two words are often confused, though their meanings are fairly easy to disentangle.

TEST YOURSELF

A. From the drained glass, the half-empty bottle of Scotch and the way Donald was stumbling around the room while the dog cringed in a corner, his wife inferred/implied that he had been drinking all afternoon.

B. Just because I look younger than my years, the policeman implied/inferred that I must have been playing truant.

C. If a man believes that he ought to do something, this implies/infers that he is physically capable of doing it.

D. It is fairly safe to imply/infer that the price of bread will rise after a poor harvest.

E. Noticing how the exotic dancer Mata Hari spent much of her time with high-ranking Allied officers, the French implied/inferred that she must be a spy, and arrested her.

F. My boss had the audacity to imply/infer that I had been dipping rather too freely into the petty cash.

G. From the way he kept glancing at me, then looking away, I implied/inferred that he was plucking up the nerve to fire me.

ANSWERS

A. *Inferred.*

B Either word could fit, depending on whether the policeman simply reached a conclusion (*inferred*) or went on to make an accusation (*implied*).

C. *Implies.*

D. *Infer.*

E. *Inferred.*

F. *Imply.*

G. *Inferred.*

Usage Tips

⚊ To *infer* means 'to make a deduction, draw an inference or reach a conclusion that is based on evidence'.

⚊ To *imply* means 'to hint, to suggest, to make an implication'. In the story *Silver Blaze,* Sherlock Holmes draws attention to the fact that a dog did not bark in the night. The great detective *infers* from its silence that the dog knew the intruder.

⚊ A handy rule of thumb is that the listener *infers* what the speaker *implies.*

⚊ In bygone years the two words were at times regarded as synonymous, and that view still has a kind of half-life, especially in America. But it makes good sense to preserve the distinction between them, and the last word on the subject may safely be left to the popular American cartoon series *The Simpsons.* Lisa Simpson, a fierce guardian of high standards, corrects a careless speaker by asserting 'You imply, I infer'.

impractical/impracticable *See* practicable/practical

index

Here's a word that has two plurals. If you are thinking of the alphabetical list of names, places and suchlike at the end of a book, the plural is *indexes*. If you have in mind mathematics, statistics and economics, the plural is *indices*.

ingenious/ingenuous

These words, though liable to be confused, point in different directions. An *ingenious* person is inventive, resourceful, full of ideas. Somebody described as *ingenuous* is open, frank, incapable of subterfuge and possibly too trusting at times.

inquiry *See* enquiry

CURIO CORNER

When an iota made a massive difference

The only difference in spelling and pronunciation between the Greek words *Homo-ousion* and *Homo-iusion* is that the second word replaces an *o* with an *i* – in Greek an *iota*. In the Byzantine Empire (AD 330–1453) that tiny difference was at the root of a life-or-death struggle. Orthodox Christians believed in *Homo-ousion*, the doctrine that God the Father and God the Son were one and the same being. Arian Christians believed just as fervently that Christ was divine but not identical with God the Father (Homoi-usion). The Orthodox believers won the argument and the Arians were persecuted as heretics. Our phrase *not an iota of difference* is a faint echo from a world in which religion permeated every aspect of life.

irregardless

Those who use this non-word are over-egging the pudding. The right word is *regardless*.

-ise

This useful little ending (usually spelled *-ize* in American English) is accepted without question in such well-established words as *nationalise, unionise, pasteurise, harmonise,* and so on, but objections have been raised to such comparative newcomers as *finalise* and *hospitalise.* There is little logic in this, but most of us feel more comfortable using the kind of language we heard when we were children. It is nevertheless worth remembering that, for the time being, *bring to an end, send to hospital* and such phrases are more acceptable to traditionalists.

issue

One of the many meanings of *issue* is 'a matter of considerable public concern'. From that starting point it has come to be a favourite word of those who, without embarrassment, use it as an official-sounding synonym for *problem* – whether the point at issue be major or petty. In which of the following examples is its use legitimate?

TEST YOURSELF

A. One of the most important issues every nation has to decide is where to strike the balance between freedom and security.

B. Although John had issues with the food they had been served he decided not to make a fuss in front of his guests.

C. We need you to work overtime every day next week. Do you have an issue with that?

D. Darren told the court he had an issue with Wayne, who had been eyeing his girlfriend on the dance floor all night.

E. There are many issues around the train service that call for attention.

ANSWERS

A. *Issues* is used correctly, but *questions* would do just as well.

B. *Issue* is too vague. Say instead *John was unhappy about the food.*

C. Again, *issue* is vague and therefore inappropriate. Say instead *Do you have any objections?*

D. Instead of using *issue* say *was annoyed by, angered by, upset by* or even *driven frantic by.*

E. *Issues around* is an even more blatant example of management-speak than *issues* on its own. Say instead *problems with.*

Usage Tips

ℹ️ *Issue* can be an unwelcome example of management-speak when it refers to matters that are of private concern, rather than public importance. To say or write *issues around* is even more off-putting for those who care about the language.

ℹ️ Alternatives, all of them more specific than the vague-sounding *issue*, include *problem, concern, worry, anxiety* and *objection.*

ĵ j j̊ ⋮ J J j j j

---

jail/gaol

British dictionaries give *gaol* as the standard spelling but allow the increasingly common *jail* in informal usage. Newspapers and magazines opt for *jail*, and in America, this is the only acceptable spelling. A computer with an American spell-checking system will mark *gaol* as incorrect.

CURIO CORNER

By Jingo!

The exclamation *By Jingo!* was originally used by conjurers, in the same way as *Hey Presto!* to draw attention to a particularly amazing trick. The use of *jingo* and *jingoism* to mean 'belligerent patriotism' was established by a music hall song of 1878, during a quarrel between Britain and Russia. Prime Minister Benjamin Disraeli's firm stance against the Russians over their attack on Turkey was given popular approval in the song:

We don't want to fight, but by Jingo if we do
We've got the ships, we've got the men, we've got the money too.

---

jejune

This word is frequently misused, mis-spelled as *jejeune* and mispronounced with a hard *j*. It comes from the Latin *jejunus* (fasting, hungry, barren) and has no direct connection with the French word *jeune* (young). The traditional meaning, 'meagre, unsatisfying, scanty', is clearly linked to the word's Latin origin, but as a consequence of an assumed French connection it has also come to be used as a synonym for 'childish, immature, puerile, callow'. Some well-respected dictionaries accept this development, but purists do not.

jetsam *See* flotsam

join together

Although the Bible pronounces: 'What, therefore, God hath joined together, let no man put asunder' the phrase *joined together* is beyond question a tautology. The idea that either people or things could be *joined apart* is plainly impossible so, weddings apart, *joined* or *join* on their own are enough without the *together*.

judgement/judgment

Either spelling is acceptable in British English. Americans usually drop the middle *e*.

k k k k **K** *k* k **k** k

---

kilometre

The preferred pronunciation is to place the accent on the first syllable: *kilo*metre – as in *kilo*gram.

Koran/Qur'an

The usual spelling in the West is *Koran*. Those seeking a spelling closer to the original Arabic prefer *Qur'an*.

CURIO CORNER

If you really want to k-now....

Have you ever thought how odd it is that *knock*, *knife*, *knight*, *knee*, *knickerbockers* and a fair number of other words are spelled with a *k* that is never pronounced? The explanation is simple: the pronunciation once followed the spelling, but the written word is far slower to accept change than the spoken word. Old English (AD 700–1150), drawing on its Germanic origins, called for the *k* to be pronounced and so, for most of its period, did Middle English (1150–1500). By the end of the 15th century, however, following the absorption of Norman French and other linguistic influences, this pronunciation had largely fallen out of fashion. If you want to blame one man for sticking to the old spelling, you need look no further than England's first printer, William Caxton (c1421–91). He spent the greater part of his working life in the Low countries, where the Germanic influence was extremely strong. When, in 1476, he set up his first press in England he brought over the typesetters whose work he knew. They chose the spellings that to their eyes seemed right and other printed books followed suit.

L

A laconic reply to a warning

An alternative name for Ancient Sparta was *Laconia*, a state whose citizens, whether referred to as Spartans or Laconians, were famous for their courage in battle, the frugality of their everyday lives and the brevity of their speech. When Philip of Macedon threatened: 'If I enter Sparta I will raze it to the ground' their *laconic* answer was: 'If.'

lamentable

By long tradition, the accent for this adjective is placed on the first syllable: **lam**entable. A modern tendency is to take a lead from the parent noun, *lament*, and say la**ment**able. This pronunciation has found its way into dictionaries as a second choice but this does not mean that it has to be encouraged.

latitude/longitude

To distinguish between these two remember that lines of latitude go across the globe and across a map. The Equator and the tropics of Cancer and Capricorn are all lines of latitude and all contain the letter *a*, a reminder of *across*. Lines of longitude run from top to bottom.

lay/lie

Even so-called quality newspapers can perpetrate one of the commonest errors in the English language and use *lay* when the right word is *lie*.

TEST YOURSELF

A. The lieutenant asked for volunteers to spy out the lay of the land.

B. When was it lain down as an unbreakable rule that it is bad manners to start eating before everybody at the table has been served?

C. In his student days, Michael seemed to be better at laying in bed than at laying plans for his career.

D. I'm so weary, I need to lay down for half an hour to recover.

E. It's only two weeks since Margery laid down grass seed but already it is sprouting.

F. There's a right way and a wrong way to lay a baby in its cot.

G. 'The best laid schemes o' mice an' men/Gang aft a-gley' (Robert Burns).

H. 'Lay that pistol down, babe!/Lay that pistol down' (1940s pop song).

I. 'Stand Up and Lay Down Sunbeds' (sign outside a tanning shop).

ANSWERS

A. Non-standard in British English. The accepted UK usage is *the lie of the land*, but a number of American authorities accept *the lay of the land* as standard.

B. Incorrect. *Laid down* is the right choice.

C. *Laying plans* is fine, but *laying in bed* should be *lying in bed*.

D. Incorrect. *Lay down* should be *lie down*.

E. Correct.

F. Correct.

G. Correct.

H. Correct.

I. Incorrect. The advertisement should read: Stand-Up and *Lie-Down* Sunbeds.

Usage Tips

ℹ️ Confusing *lay* and *lie* is fairly common, and not just in regional dialects. The verb *to lay*, meaning to put, place or prepare, takes a direct object – that is, there must always be something that is laid. A hen lays an egg, you lay the table, lay down the law, lay your plans and so on. The verb *to lie*, when it means to recline or be at rest, does not take a direct object. You lie in bed, a book lies open, a secret lies hidden.

ℹ️ So far, so simple. But confusion creeps in because *lay* is not only a verb in its own right but also the past tense of *lie*: *I lay awake for hours last night*.

ℹ️ The past participles of *lie* and *lay* (a participle is simply a part of the verb) are fairly easy to confuse, too. All you need to remember is that *lain* is the past participle of *lie* and *laid* is the past participle of *lay*. So it's *I have lain in bed long enough*, but *I laid my cards on the table last night*.

ℹ️ There are just two exceptions to the rule that *lay* takes a direct object: hens and ships. A farmer may say that his hens are laying well, without saying what they are laying, since it could only be eggs. And a ship can lay alongside or lay forward.

CURIO CORNER

A leading question

In the legal world, where the phrase originated, a *leading question* is one framed in a way that will produce the desired answer. A lawyer may ask a witness: 'Did you see the accused man smash a bottle and jab it into my client's face?' A non-leading way of putting the question would be: 'What did you see after the accused man walked up to the bar?' Outside the courts, the phrase is often used – or rather, misused – to mean an awkward question, intended to produce an incriminating or embarrassing answer. A banker, asked why charges were going up at a time when the bank was making record profits, might play for time by saying: 'That's a leading question.'

legend/legendary

A legend is a story based on fact or on folk memory that is often embroidered with additions that add to a person's fame but are not necessarily true. It is legitimate to describe Robin Hood as legendary but to apply the same term to Don Bradman is to weaken its meaning. His reputation as a batsman is based entirely on fact, and all the important facts, from his 6,996 runs in 52 Test matches to his total of 28,057 in first class cricket, are on record. The phrase *A legend in his/her own lifetime* has become a cliché that is best avoided.

lend/loan

Can you imagine Mark Antony demanding: 'Friends, Romans, country-men, loan me your ears!'? Yet the increasingly frequent use of the noun *loan* in place of the verb *lend* is no longer as wholeheartedly condemned as once it was. Which of the following sentences, in your opinion, use *loan* incorrectly?

TEST YOURSELF

A. Britain was close to bankruptcy after the Second World War, but America came to the rescue with a $3.75 billion loan that had strings attached.
B. Can you loan me your pen to sign this Get Well card?
C. It was quite a coup for the Royal Academy when the Russians agreed to loan it a selection of near-priceless paintings for an exhibition.
D. 'Boy, 8, loans explicit book from school' (newspaper headline).
E. Our local library loans out books for as long as three weeks.

ANSWERS

A. *Loan* is correct.
B. *Lend* is the right choice.
C. Both *lend* and *loan* are acceptable.
D. Time was when sub-editing a national newspaper without due care and attention was a near-capital crime. But here, the word *loans* conveys the exact opposite of what was intended, and nobody, from the editor down, seems to have noticed. The right word is *borrows*.

E. *Lends* is preferable to *loans*.

Usage Tips

ℹ️ *Lend* is a verb – an action word – and *loan* is a noun – a naming word. But despite the annoyance it can cause to careful speakers, *loan* is increasingly being used as a verb. This usage is more strongly established in North America than in Britain.

ℹ️ If you want to use *loan* as a verb it is better to reserve it for transactions that are fairly weighty – as, for example, in Sentence **C**. For more trivial matters, such as borrowing a pen or issuing library books, *lend* is the better choice.

less *See* fewer

like/as if/such as

The word *like* can come trippingly off the tongue or keyboard, even when it is technically incorrect. But widespread and rapidly increasing use has made tolerable what was once almost unthinkable. Which of the following sentences would upset a purist, and how would you change them?

TEST YOURSELF

A. 'He made me look, and feel, like I was serving under-arm' (US tennis player Taylor Dent, paying tribute to Andy Murray's service returns).

B. It looks like the 10.45 train is going to be late again.

C. Mathematicians, like poets, often do their best work before they reach the age of 30.

D. The pools winner who announced she was going to 'Spend, spend, spend' got through her winnings like there was no tomorrow.

E. 'Like most professional models her toes are covered with bunions and malformed' (Evelyn Waugh).

F. 'This letter explains why offenders like John Amery had to be prosecuted' (Rebecca West).

G. 'When I first read Dostoevsky I was – Hey, like, Wow!' (college student).

H. I'd like for you to try these new tablets, because they certainly worked for me.

I. I was like 'Don't try to get round me with that old line' and he was like 'No, I really mean it'.

J. I didn't want to butt in, like, where I wasn't wanted.

K. 'Her forlorn attempts to mime the words reminded me irresistibly of poor old John Redmond, as Welsh Secretary, trying and failing to make it look like he knew the words to the Welsh National Anthem' (*Daily Telegraph*).

L. 'Like human males, the fights (between elephant seals) stem from one of two causes – land or ladies' (*The Spectator*).

M. 'I feel like I can share this with you' (BBC's *Radio 5 Live*).

ANSWERS

A. Replace *like I was* with *as if I were* or *as though I were*.

B. Replace *like* with *as if*.

C. *Like* is correct.

D. Informally, *like* is acceptable. *As if there were no tomorrow* would be correct, but in this context it sounds pedantic.

E. Despite Waugh's stature as a writer, a rewrite is needed: *Her toes, like those of most professional models...*

F. *Like* is fine, even though some traditionalists would prefer *such as*.

G. The student's command of grammar falls short of her enthusiasm. Try: *I was astounded*.

H. Delete *for*.

I. This way of dropping *like* into a sentence, in place of such phrases as *I said* and *he replied,* began as a vogue among American teenagers. The best that can be said about it is that it is lively, but it was never good grammar and it's beginning to look dated.

J. *Like* is redundant, but this usage can crop up in some local dialects.

K. Replace *like* with *as if* or *as though*.

L. Replace *like* with *as among* or *as with*.

M. Delete *like* or replace it with *as if* or *as though*. And *share,* in the way it is used, is management-speak.

Usage Tips

[i] Sticklers maintain that when *like* means 'similar to' or 'in the same way as' it is acceptable only if it is followed by a noun – as in *Usain Bolt ran like the wind*. It pains them to see it followed by a complete phrase – as in *Usain Bolt ran like he believed nobody on earth could beat him*. Bolt had a point, and so do the sticklers.

[i] You are not likely to go wrong if you use *as, as if, as though* or *such as* in place of *like* whenever it sounds right to do so.

[i] There are times when idiom is stronger than any rule. It would be harsh to object to usages such as *run like mad* and *like there was no tomorrow*.

[i] Some authorities still rule out *like* altogether when it introduces examples and recommend replacing it with *such as*. Others accept *like* if only one example follows but advise using *such as* if there are more than one. It is hard to see the logic in accepting *songwriters like John Lennon*, but rejecting *songwriters like John Lennon and Paul McCartney*. Insisting on *such as* instead of *like* in such cases is now regarded as an old-fashioned prejudice, but it is well to be aware of it.

[i] In America and in Australia the use of *like* to mean 'in the same way as' is acceptable in all but the most formal speech and writing.

listen up!

The American way of alerting people in a crisp and authoritative way that an announcement is about to be made has gained a firm foothold in Britain. But *Listen up!* in place of the quieter *Here is an announcement* is not condoned by careful speakers.

literally

Asked whether a downturn in the economy had harmed the sales of luxury foods, an assistant buyer at Fortnum & Mason gave a buoyant answer: 'Grouse has been literally flying off the shelf.' Quite a trick, considering that the birds had been shot, gutted, hung, plucked and trussed to make them ready for the oven. In most of the sentences below, *literally* is misused. How would you correct them?

TEST YOURSELF
A. It's so hot on the beach today that I'm literally roasting.
B. After Edmund Hillary and Norgay Tenzing came down from conquering Mount Everest they found themselves literally up to their necks in messages of congratulation.
C. I have literally reached the end of my patience with shoppers who keep me waiting while they fumble for their money at the supermarket till.
D. The young curate spared no effort in getting to know his flock. He was literally a father to every child within miles.
E. 'I'm suffocating here without active work to do, literally suffocating' (Josef Stalin, writing from exile in 1908).
F. Jenny was literally over the moon when she saw her examination results.
G. With a perfect seven iron out of the rough, McIlroy landed his ball literally two inches from the pin.
H. Class 3C lived up to their reputation for being beyond control, and before his first week was up their new teacher was literally at the end of his tether.
I. 'They were literally queuing up to apologise' (BBC interviewee).

ANSWERS
A. Delete *literally* and try *practically*.
B. Delete literally and try *almost*.
C. No change is needed.
D. Just wait until his bishop hears about this! Replace *literally* with *virtually*, *figuratively*, *metaphorically* or *regarded as* to make it clear that the curate was above suspicion.
E. The world might have been a happier place had the young Stalin's statement been literally true.
F. Delete *literally*.
G. Delete *literally*. It is grammatically correct, but unnecessary for it adds nothing to the meaning.

H. Unless the teacher had been tethered to a stake – which is unlikely even with the worst-behaved class in the land – *literally* is misused here.

I. Delete *literally*. As in Sentence **G**, it is not needed.

Usage Tips

ℹ️ *Literally*, one of the most misused words in the language, should be kept in solitary confinement and allowed out only when it is needed in statements that are meant to be taken as nothing but the unvarnished truth.

ℹ️ Avoid the temptation to use *literally* merely to add emphasis.

loan *See* lend

lose out

This American import is increasingly heard in Britain, despite resistance from those who believe a simple *lose* is enough. It is hard to side with the view that adding *out* never makes a difference. Take, for instance a statement such as *Children who do not take enough exercise in their school years will lose out in later life*. Omit *out,* and the question is raised: what will they lose? Put it back and it becomes clear that they will lose opportunities to improve their chances in life.

M

Mahomet *See* **Muhammad**

man *See* **sexist language**

mate

It can be irritating to be addressed as 'mate' by somebody who cannot claim close friendship. *Mate* is a term of endearment, not only in certain regions but throughout the country. The very word *workmate* suggests companionship. This is precisely why many people find it objectionable to be addressed as *mate* by somebody who is not a close friend and may even be a total stranger.

may/might

These two are sometimes interchangeable but when they are not they can easily be confused.

TEST YOURSELF

A. I may/might be able to have lunch with you next Tuesday, but I'll have to check my diary.

B. It may/might come as news to you, waiter, but we've been sitting at this table for at least half an hour and still nobody has come to take our order.

C. England's hopes of retaining the Ashes may/might have a better chance of success if we could somehow find another Compton, another Trueman or another Botham.

D. John made a promise that he intended to keep, come what may/might.

E. May/might I trouble you to pass the salt?

F. Whatever mistakes you may/might have made in your last job, you now have the chance to prove that you are 100 per cent reliable.

G. If the accused driver had not been talking on his mobile phone he may/might have seen the lorry in time.

H. I may/might have got away with the disguise if my false moustache had not slipped off at a crucial moment.

I. You may/might have offered to give me a hand when you saw me struggling with all that heavy shopping.

ANSWERS

A. Either word could be chosen, with *may* suggesting a stronger likelihood of a lunch meeting than *might*.

B. Again, either word could be used, but this time *might* conveys a stronger rebuke than *may*.

C. Since the speaker clearly believes that England's chances of retaining the Ashes are remote, *might* is a better choice than *may*.

D. *May.*

E. *Might* is a shade more polite than *may*.

F. *May* is the better choice. *Might* opens up the possibility that some mistakes could have been made but were not.

G. *Might.*

H. *Might.*

I. *Might* is by far the more likely choice. *May have offered* opens up the possibility that help was in fact offered.

Usage Tips

ℹ️ When referring to the possibility that something has happened, is happening or will happen, *may* usually suggests a stronger likelihood than *might*.

ℹ️ When making a request, *might* is a shade more polite than *may*.

ℹ️ *Can I* is not regarded as an acceptable substitute for *may I* or *might I* because it could easily be taken as a question about the speaker's ability to carry out an act, rather than a request for permission.

ℹ️ *Might* can sometimes convey a rebuke with a slightly sarcastic undertone, as in Sentence **B**.

medalled

If a fashion model can be said to *model*, why should a medal-winning athlete not be allowed to *medal*? Dame Tanni Grey-Thompson, Britain's celebrated Paralympian athlete, has been quoted as saying: 'The reality – and it is surely not right at the moment – is that you have to *multi-medal* at the Paralympic Games to get a New Year's Honours list award.' Not everybody who agrees with her sentiments will find it easy to accept her choice of words. Most people who care about the language do not condone this modern example of a noun masquerading as a verb. Even so, it has established a firm foothold in sports reporting and appears to have been accepted by the BBC. Purists are determined that the foothold should not become a bridgehead.

media

A handy way of referring to television, radio, newspapers, magazines and the internet can be to regard them as a single entity – the *media*. This does not mean that the noun *media* should be treated as if it were singular.

TEST YOUSELF
A. The British media was/were united in its/their enthusiastic support for Joanna Lumley when she championed the cause of the Gurkhas.
B. The media has/have demonstrated that it knows/they know how to put the government on the defensive, or even force it to make a U-turn.
C. It has to be accepted that the internet has become almost as powerful a media/medium of mass communication as television.

ANSWERS
A. *Were* and *their*   **B.** *Have* and *they*   **C.** *Medium*

Usage Tips

ⓘ Purists maintain that it is incorrect to treat *media* as a singular word because it is the plural of the Latin word *medium*. Nevertheless, it is often used in the singular, and those who do so can point to the undeniable fact that English does not always follow the rules of Latin. In support of this line of reasoning they could cite the word *agenda*. Using this word in the singular, now universally accepted, was once strongly discouraged, because it is the plural form of the Latin *agendum*.

ⓘ For all that, the day that *media* follows the lead of *agenda* has not yet arrived. Until then it is safer to use it only as plural.

ⓘ When *medium* is used to refer to the arts or to somebody who seeks to contact the spirit world, its plural is *mediums*.

meet/with/up/up with

To British ears, especially those of the older generation, *with* and *up* can sound like uninvited guests when they follow *meet*. Are they acceptable in the sentences below?

TEST YOURSELF
A. Why don't we *meet up* for a drink some day next week?
B. The architect's plans for new council offices *met with* instant approval.
C. The chief executive of the company *met with* the sales team to go over the figures.
D. John and Sally arranged to *meet up with* their friends before going to the pub.
E. The General was willing to *meet with* anybody who had the authority to sign an armistice.

ANSWERS
A. *Meet* is sufficient by itself, but *meet up* is acceptable in informal speech.
B. *Met with* is well established in this usage.
C. *Met with* is intended to make the meeting sound important, but *with* is not necessary.
D. *Meet up with* is taking informality too far and will annoy traditionalists.
E. *Meet* is preferable, but *meet with* is acceptable.

Usage Tips

ℹ️ For many years the verb *meet* stood on its own, without any need for assistance. Then, following an American lead, some people began to *meet with* their friends or arranged to *meet up*. A hard core of traditionalists in Britain objected vigorously to the extra words, on the grounds that they added nothing to the meaning. But it can be argued that both *we met up* and *we met with* carry a strong implication that the meeting was not simply by chance, whereas a simple *we met* leaves that possibility open.

ℹ️ The best advice is to remember the old adage: when in doubt, leave it out. Try to avoid *meet with* and *meet up* unless you are sure that the extra words add something to the meaning. And steer clear of *meet up with,* because it uses one word too many.

militate/mitigate

The two are confused with surprising frequency.

TEST YOURSELF

A. The prisoner admitted he was drunk when he smashed the jeweller's window, in the fond belief that this admission would militate/mitigate his punishment.

B. Rationing is perhaps the best way to militate against/mitigate widespread distress when food supplies run short.

C. The gravity of the crisis militates against/mitigates hopes for a swift recovery.

D. A period of silence from you would go a long way towards militating against/mitigating my displeasure at your conduct.

E. The goalkeeper's casual attitude towards training militated against/ mitigated choosing him as a starter in important games.

ANSWERS

A. *Mitigate* **B.** *Mitigate* **C.** *Militates against*
D. *Mitigating* **E.** *Militated against*

Usage Tips

ℹ️ To *mitigate* means 'to reduce in force, intensity or severity'. A young prisoner in the dock, for example, might offer in *mitigation* the plea that he was under the influence of older companions.

ℹ️ To *militate against* means 'to fight against a proposal or assertion, using forceful evidence'. If you think of the word *military* you are unlikely to make mistakes with *militate.*

ⓘ A common mistake is to use such phrases as *this mitigates against*. The best way to avoid this is never to follow *mitigate* with *against*.

millennium

The correct spelling is with a double *l* and a double *n*. Think of *million* and *annual*.

misrelated phrases *See* backing into sentences

momentarily

In British English this word means '*for* a moment', as in 'I paused *momentarily*, to straighten my tie'. In American English it means '*in* a moment', as in 'Take a seat. I'll be with you *momentarily*.'

moment in time

Since time is made up of moments and moment means 'a brief period or a specific point in time' the phrase '*a moment in time*' is an example of redundancy. It is encountered too often, and belongs in the wastepaper basket of ready-made howlers. Often the single word *now* will do the job.

Moslem/Muslim

The spelling preferred by those followers of Islam who live in English-speaking countries is *Muslim*.

Muhammad/Mohammad/Mahomet

In an attempt to bring the Western spelling closer to the Arabic pronunciation there is now general agreement that the name of the founder of Islam should be spelled *Muhammad*. More than three centuries ago the original European spelling, *Mahomet,* began to be replaced by *Mohammed,* and now this in turn had been superseded. When the heavyweight champion who began his career in the ring as Cassius Clay decided to take on a Muslim name he chose *Muhammad Ali.*

CURIO CORNER

Mutual friends

In the eyes of ultra-purists Charles Dickens made an error when he used the title *Our Mutual Friend*. It should, they claim, have been *Our Common Friend* or *The Friend We Have in Common*. But the first of these suggestions could imply that the friend was uncouth or, even worse in the eyes of respectable Victorian citizens, a member of the lower orders. And the second is unwieldy. Strictly speaking, *mutual* should be applied only when what is held in common works both ways – *mutual admiration*, for example. It could be argued, though, that *mutual friend,* apart from having Dickens's seal of approval, has been around long enough to earn its place in the language.

myself

Think twice before using *myself*. It can add emphasis as in 'I myself take full responsibility for the under-cooked chicken'. But more frequently the word will be redundant or make a statement seem pompous. Oscar Wilde would have shown just as much wit if he had eliminated *myself* when he wrote: 'Perhaps, after all, America never has been discovered. I myself would say that it had merely been detected.' It is also a good idea to be wary of *himself, herself, yourself, themselves, ourselves* and *yourselves*.

n n n n N n n n

neither

Should *neither* take a singular verb or a plural one? And does the traditional view still hold, that *neither nor* should be used only when two possible outcomes are being rejected? See also **either**.

TEST YOURSELF

A. Despite months of hard training, neither Wilson nor one of his team mates are likely to break the Olympic record.

B. Neither Joan nor her sisters are desperate to sell the house, so they will probably stay put.

C. This so-called master-plan of yours is neither fish nor fowl nor good red herring.

D. I neither approve of your money-making scheme or intend to take any part in it.

E. The Cabinet minister who bears the proud title of Lord Privy Seal is neither a lord nor a privy nor a seal – nor even always a male.

F. Neither the Clantons nor Wyatt Earp and his partners were likely to back away from a fight at the OK Corral.

ANSWERS
A. Incorrect. *Are likely* should be *is likely.*
B. Correct.
C. Acceptable, even though it ignores the 'two possibilities only' rule.
D. Incorrect. *Or intend* should be *nor intend.*
E. Acceptable. To apply the 'two only' rule would spoil the joke.
F. Correct.

Usage Tips

ⓘ If both possibilities are singular, as in Sentence **A**, *neither* takes a singular verb. If both are plural, as in Sentence **F**, the verb is plural. If one is singular and the other plural, the verb should match the possibility that is nearest to it – as in Sentence **B**.

ⓘ In the case of idioms and other long-established phrases, as in Sentences **C** and **E**, the 'two only' rule can safely be ignored.

ⓘ *Neither* should be balanced by *nor* – never, as in Sentence **D**, by *or.*

ⓘ If more than two possible outcomes are rejected, the 'two only' rule can often be sidestepped by using such words as *none, not any* or *not one.*

ⓘ The preferred way of pronouncing *neither* is to rhyme the first syllable with rye, but *neether* has become generally acceptable in informal speech.

none
Does this word take a singular verb or is it plural? Or could it be either?

TEST YOURSELF
A. 'None but the brave deserve/deserves the fair' (John Dryden).
B. None of the songs in the new musical is/are tuneful enough to stay in the memory for more than a few minutes after the curtain falls.

C. There were three experienced strikers in the local football team, but none of them was/were eager to step forward and take penalties.

D. I searched the box but to my disappointment none of the chisels inside was/were sharp enough to do its/their job properly.

E. I had five £20 notes in my wallet yesterday, but after last night's poker session, none of them is/are left.

F. Where do you keep the potatoes? I've looked high and low but it's beginning to look as if there are/is none in the house.

ANSWERS

A. *Deserves*.

B. *Is*.

C. Strictly speaking, *was*. But *were* is acceptable informally.

D. *Was* and *its* are preferable to *were* and *their*.

E. *None are left* is correct, but a possible alternative is *not one of them is left*.

F. *Are*.

Usage Tips

[i] The general rule is that *none* is singular, and this is certainly the case when, as in Sentences **A** and **B**, it means *nobody*, *no one* or *not a single one*.

[i] If *none* is intended to mean *not any*, as in Sentences **E** and **F**, it takes a plural verb.

[i] When *none* could mean either *not one* or *not any*, as in Sentences **C** and **D**, it is usually safe to regard it as being singular.

no one

No hyphen is needed.

non-sequitur

This Latin phrase, meaning 'it does not follow', is applied to conclusions that do not follow logically from what has just been stated. How would you get rid of the non-sequiturs below?

TEST YOURSELF

A. Born in 1961, Mary spent her early years in Chislehurst.

B. Brought up never to tell a lie, George Washington is said to have chopped down his father's cherry tree.

C. World -famous as a violinist in her early teens, Julia gave up smoking when she reached the age of 30.

D. Advertised goods *must* be good.

ANSWERS

The following are suggested alternatives:

A. Mary, who was born in 1961, spent her early years in Chislehurst.

B. George Washington was brought up never to tell a lie, and is said to have owned up after chopping down his father's cherry tree.

C. Julia became world famous as a violinist in her early teens. When she reached the age of 30 she gave up smoking.

D. The only way to get rid of the illogicality in this statement is not to make it in the first place.

Usage Tip

🛈 There are two main causes of non-sequiturs: packing too much information into a sentence and trying to introduce variety by occasionally copying a Latin way of constructing sentences. See also **backing into sentences**.

not un-

George Orwell had a strong dislike for the *not un-* construction. He held it up to ridicule with his parody: *A not unblack dog was chasing a not unsmall rabbit across a not ungreen field.* Orwell had a point, and it is *not unlikely* that other writers of his day used the *not un-* construction too freely. Even so, it can be useful at times. Nor is it unthinkable to reject advice, even from a source as revered as the author of *Animal Farm* and *1984*.

(O) O ◎ ⊡ **O** 𝟬 ◇ ◆ O

oblivious

The rule used to be: *oblivious of* and never *oblivious to*. Today, both forms have more or less equal standing. Even so, avoid *oblivious to* if you want to have the purists on your side.

of course

It sounds entirely logical that if there is no reason for doubt, there is no need to say *of course*. Nor is there any question that the phrase pops up far too freely. These are reasons for using it thoughtfully, but not for banning it totally.

TEST YOURSELF
A. Are you with me in this struggle or not? Of course I am.
B. It will, of course, take longer for the kettle to boil up here, since the mountain is more than 5,000 metres high.
C. We are still friends, of course, so let's have no more squabbling.
D. 'You praise the firm restraint with which they write –
I'm with you there, of course:
They use the snaffle and the curb all right,
But where's the bloody horse?'
(Roy Campbell)

ANSWERS
A. *Of course* adds emphasis and enthusiasm, so it is acceptable.
B. *Of course* adds nothing, so it is not needed.
C. *Of course* is on the borderline. Take it away and not much is lost to the meaning. Leave it in and it could be justified because it underlines the friendship.

D. Strictly speaking, *of course* is not needed. But it helps the rhythm and adds a slight emphasis. In any case, the poet needed a rhyme for *horse*.

Usage Tip

ℹ Think before you use *of course* and if it adds nothing to the meaning, give the phrase a rest.

off of

Do not be misled by the phrasing in the song that goes: *You're just too good to be true./Can't take my eyes off of you.*

Off of is never likely to win a place in standard English. A simple *off* is enough.

oligarch

A fair number of Western reporters and columnists find it hard to understand how a handful of Russians managed to pull themselves out of near poverty and amassed colossal riches following the break-up of the Soviet system. The same columnists, it appears, find it just as hard to use their mother tongue properly, for they cannot resist describing the enterprising Russians as *oligarchs*. The word *oligarchy* means 'government by the few', not 'government by the rich'. Some of Russia's overnight billionaires are so far from ruling as oligarchs that they have served or are serving time in jail. Others, with football clubs and huge businesses to run, already have more than enough claims on their time and energy.

one

Unless you are a member of the royal family or have pretensions to belong to the upper crust, using *one* instead of such words as *you, I, we* or *people* may well invite ridicule. There may still be occasions when you have no alternative – as the jazz pianist Fats Waller said, *One never knows, do one?* Try to keep them to a minimum.

one another *See* **each other**

ongoing

It is difficult to think of an occasion when *ongoing* adds anything to the meaning. What is the difference between an *ongoing investigation* and a plain *investigation*? Between an *inquiry* and an *ongoing inquiry*? Or between a *problem* and an *ongoing problem*? There is always a strong presumption, unless it is stated that a conclusion has been reached, that the *investigations, inquiries* and *problems* are still going on. *Ongoing* is usually off-putting and even if it is necessary to stress that nothing has been brought to a conclusion, *continuing* is a friendlier, far less bureaucratic-sounding choice.

only

This word has probably given more joy to pedants on the lookout for examples of wrongful usage than any other word in the language. Its position in a sentence can introduce ambiguity or alter the meaning. Rightly – that is to say, logically – placed, it can sometimes sound awkward. Try shifting the position of *only* in the sentence: *I went to the shops only yesterday* and you will find that every move creates a new meaning or a different emphasis.

TEST YOURSELF
- **A.** If only you would listen to your mother you might change your attitude.
- **B.** 'Drink to me only with thine eyes,/And I will pledge with mine' (Ben Jonson).
- **C.** 'I Only Have Eyes for You' (popular song of the 1930s).
- **D.** Michael will only drink a dry white wine with fish.
- **E.** I will only take a tea break when I have finished the job.
- **F.** Margaret was only able to give a few pence to the church roof appeal because she had lost her purse.
- **G.** If only John had been warned about the strength of the undertow the tragedy might never have happened.

H. David knew it was only a matter of time before his hiding place would be discovered.

ANSWERS

A. Sentence A is fine as it stands. A pedant might point out that *only you* implies *nobody else but you*. But then the sentence would no longer make sense.

B. If grammar and logic were all that mattered, the positioning of *only* could be criticised as inviting ambiguity. It could in theory be taken to mean *Drink to me and to nobody else*. Yet the true meaning is beyond doubt. No change is needed.

C. Only eyes? Not arms, lips or even a heart? Strictly speaking, *only* should come after *eyes*. Yet no change is needed in the sequence of words. The meaning is clear, and moving *only* would throw out the rhythm of the song. But do not take this as a reason to ignore grammar when writing prose.

D. Only *drink* the wine? Not pour it on to the carpet? Logically, *only* should follow *drink*. But no change is needed. The meaning is clear as the sentence stands, and the strictly grammatical version, placing *only* after *drink*, would sound pedantic.

E. Only take a tea break? Not, for instance, dance around the room or ask for a pay rise? Although the meaning is clear, it would be better to avoid even the possibility of ambiguity by saying: *Only when I have finished the job will I take a tea break*.

F. The sentence is perfectly clear as it stands. The word *only* could be shifted to come after *give*, but this would make no difference to the sense.

G. *If only John* could be taken to mean *if nobody else but John*. Rewrite: *If John had only been warned*.

H. *Only* is correctly placed.

Usage Tips

ⓘ When it comes to placing *only* in a sentence, much depends on whether you take a pedantic or a permissive view. Strict grammarians have logic on their side when they maintain that it should always come as close as possible to the word or phrase it refers to – as in Sentence **H**. Those who disagree say that the meaning is often perfectly clear when *only* is placed in a more natural-sounding position, as in Sentence **F**.

[i] Perhaps the best approach is to veer towards putting *only* in its logical place when speaking or writing formally and towards selecting its 'natural' place when the context is informal. Be aware, though, that purists may pounce on placings which to you may seem informal and acceptable but to them appear to be careless and casual.

opposite

Should it be *opposite to, opposite from* or *opposite of*?

TEST YOURSELF
A. Your view of the problem is the exact opposite to/from/of mine.
B. You seem to have fallen into a habit of automatically taking a view that is opposite to/from/of mine.
C. The two old friends placed their deck chairs opposite to/from/of each other.

ANSWERS
A. *Of;* an alternative would be to say *exactly opposite to mine.*
B. *To* and *from* are both acceptable.
C Sometimes, as in Sentence **C**, *opposite* needs no preposition.

Usage Tips
[i] When *opposite* is used as a noun, as in Sentence **A**, it should normally be followed by *of*. Using *to* can also be acceptable, but only in informal speech and writing.
[i] When *opposite* is used as an adjective, as in Sentence **B**, either *to* or *from* is correct.

optimal, optimum

Both words are widely but incorrectly used as if they meant *the best* or *the maximum*. Their true meaning is: *the best that can be expected, taking all the circumstances into account.* The *optimum* result for workers on strike for a six per cent pay rise might be to get what they were asking for, whereas an *optimal* result, taking into account the hardships and financial losses associated with going on strike, might be a settlement at, say, four per cent.

ordinance/ordnance

Both words come from the Latin *ordinare,* to put in order, which perhaps explains why, although they have different meanings, they are easily confused. An *ordinance* is an official order or a religious rite. *Ordnance* means artillery – both guns and ammunition. To remember the difference between the two words, think of the Ordnance Survey maps. They were originally drawn up by the Army to help in the siting of artillery, to defend the nation against a possible invasion.

CURIO CORNER

When it really hit home to be ostracised

In the eyes of the Ancient Greeks and Ancient Romans one of the worst of all punishments was for a man to be banished from his city. It was a penalty reserved for those who were considered a danger to the State, and it could last for 10 years. Such a weighty decision had to be taken by a majority of citizens, who cast their votes by writing the miscreant's name on a shell or a shard of broken pottery and casting it into a large pot. The Greek word for a shard was *ostrakon* and the process of banishment was *ostrakismos.* The present-day meaning of *ostracise* owes much to the original word, but the misery of being excluded from a group, shunned by friends and neighbours and being 'sent to Coventry' is perhaps not quite as bitter as 10 years of banishment.

---

orient/orientate

In British usage the two words have become more or less interchangeable: *I'm beginning to orient/orientate myself towards your side of the argument.* Americans prefer to stick to *orient.*

out

The Scots, with characteristic economy of words, use such phrases as *the dog wants out,* leaving the words *to go* unspoken but implied. The same economical use of language is seen when conspirators in a plot decide the time has come to break with their companions. 'I want out' may be a clear statement of intention, but it is not standard English.

overly

In North America and to some extent in Scotland, *overly* is used where standard British usage calls for *over.* An American mother might be *overly protective* of her children; an English parent would be *over-protective.*

owing to *See* due to

P p P ⠏ P p p p

paradigm

The word has entered business jargon from science and grammatical studies and is now freely used in such macho expressions as *I'm determined to bust the paradigm!* All this means is that the speaker intends to challenge a belief or opinion that is widely held.

parameter

Originally a mathematical term, *parameter* has became a vogue word that is called upon when somebody is seeking an important-sounding substitute for such everyday terms as *limit, boundary, edge* or *restraint.*

passed/past

An examination can be *passed* or failed, but once over it is in the *past.* A marathon runner will have *passed* all rivals leaving some to be consoled, perhaps, by memories of their *past* triumphs.

TEST YOURSELF

A. It's time to start thinking about tomorrow. There's no point in living in the past/passed.

B. It was well passed/past their bedtime, but the children were still up, playing computer games.

C. Despite all his doubts and uncertainties beforehand, Michael past/passed the examination with flying colours.

D. A skein of geese in V-formation past/passed high overhead, honking noisily.

E. A flurry of good news in the financial pages suggested that the recession had past/passed.

ANSWERS

A. *Past*   **B.** *Past*   **C.** *Passed*   **D.** *Passed*   **E.** *Passed*

Usage Tips

ℹ️ *Passed* is a verb (*The relay team passed the baton faultlessly*).

ℹ️ *Past* can be a noun (*It happened long ago, in the distant past*), an adjective (*Her past successes were eclipsed in the final examinations*) or an adverb (*The postman hurried past our house because he thought our dog was more likely to sink its teeth into him than to wag its tail*).

peninsula/peninsular

Without the *r* it's a noun, denoting a piece of land bounded on three sides by water: *the Gower peninsula*. Add an *r* and it's an adjective: *Wellington made his name as a military commander in the Peninsular War*.

per cent

Beware of the candidate who promises: 'If you hire me I'll give the job 110 per cent.' He or she has a less than 100 per cent grasp of English. Nor is this the only pitfall set for the unwary by these two little words.

TEST YOURSELF

A. Only a percentage of those who voted for Margaret Thatcher in 1979 had an inkling of just how formidable she would turn out to be.

B. If you are playing the Old Course at St Andrew's on a windy day it pays to weigh up the percentages with every shot you take.

C. What per cent will come my way if your project turns out to be a great success?

D. In the Soviet era the term Stakhanovite was coined to signify outstanding effort and productivity. It was a tribute to the prodigious capacity for work shown by the miner Alexei Stakhanov, who never put in less than 200 per cent of effort.

ANSWERS

A. Wrong. A *percentage*, with no qualifying adjective, is not necessarily low. The addition of *small* would bring out the intended meaning.

B. Correct.

C. Wrong. The word should be *percentage*.

D. Wrong. It is impossible, by definition, to put in more than more than 100 per cent of effort. Stakhanov's achievement was that, according to the Soviet authorities, he and his team increased coal production sevenfold. That amounts to 700 per cent of output, a result which could perhaps have been achieved only through an unsurpassable 100 per cent of effort.

Usage Tips

i A percentage can be high, medium or small, and the writer should say which is intended. In Sentence **A** what is meant is a *small percentage*.

i *Percentage* in the sense of 'a small gain or advantage' is not usually standard English but this usage is acceptable in the fields of sport and finance. *Percent is* written as one word in America but as two – *per cent* – in Britain.

ℹ A profit or a loss can amount to 200 per cent, 300 per cent or anything higher within reason. But an effort or a commitment can never be more than 100 per cent.

persuade *See* convince

phenomena/phenomenon

It is a sign of a neglected education to speak of *a phenomena,* for this is a plural word. The singular form is *phenomenon.* Another fairly common error is to reach too readily for the word when something less spectacular is needed. A sales campaign that achieves results only slightly above the ordinary cannot be accurately described as a *phenomenal* success. Say *a complete* or *an encouraging success* instead.

pour/pore

You can *pour* yourself and your friends a drink, *pour* oil over troubled waters, *pour* your heart out over a lost love. But you cannot, unless you are splashing the drink about in a clumsy way, *pour* over a book, a letter or a document. The word for concentrating intensely on reading the written word Is *poring.*

practicable/practical

These words clearly have a common origin, and their meanings are close enough to lead occasionally to uncertainty about which to use.

TEST YOURSELF
A. Dozens of theories have been put forward about the identity of Jack the Ripper but for all practical/practicable purposes it has to be accepted that the mystery will never be solved.
B. Is it entirely impractical/impracticable to expect a builder to wait until he finishes the job before putting in his final bill?
C. Very few practical/practicable suggestions have been made about ways of attracting mass audiences back into the habit of going to the cinema every week.

D. Raymond's big idea for restoring the family's fortune seemed attractive at first, but it turned out not to be practical/practicable.

ANSWERS
A. *Practical*   **B**. *Impracticable*   **C**. *Practical*   **D**. *Practicable*

Usage Tips

ℹ️ A *practical* person is one who sets a higher value on experience than on abstract theories, and so makes a habit of getting things done. A *practical* idea is one that provides the solution to a problem. Synonyms for *practical* include *useful, sensible, efficient, skilful, businesslike* and *down-to-earth*.

ℹ️ A plan or an idea that is *practicable* is one that is capable of being carried out. Synonyms for *practicable* include *achievable, feasible, workable, likely* and *attainable*.

practically

Purists frown on the use of *practically* to mean 'almost' – as in *I had practically given up hope*. Any justification these objections may once have had is fading as the years go by.

prepositions at the end of a sentence

Grammarians in the 17th century tried to impose a rule that it was poor English to write a sentence that ended with a preposition. They took their cue from Latin, in which *praepositio* (preposition) means 'placed before'. It followed, so they said, that prepositions – *at, by, from, for, to, with* and so on – should not be placed after other words in the same sentence. Such was the prestige of Latin that generations of school-teachers took up the cry. Instead of *That's a proposal I cannot agree with*, anybody aspiring to use the language correctly was expected to say or write *That's a proposal with which I cannot agree*. The prohibition was never well founded, for English, although it owes a massive debt to Latin, has developed in its own way. Outside the classroom, the committee room and the council chamber the 'rule' has generally been ignored. Winston Churchill sounded its death knell when he commented on a report written by an ambitious but unfortunate junior: 'This is the sort of English up with which I will not put.'

CURIO CORNER

Prestige from conjuring tricks

When it first came into the language the word *prestige* was associated with illusions, sleight of hand and conjuring tricks. It is derived from the Latin *praestringere*, meaning 'to dazzle, to bind up, to blindfold' – all of them effects that could be brought about by a spellbinding display of conjuring. When *prestige* and *prestigious* first came into English they brought with them more than a whiff of trickery, but the notion of dazzling proved to be even stronger. All the negative associations have long fallen away, and prestige is now seen only as the reward for some outstanding quality or performance.

prevaricate, procrastinate

Confusion between these two is widespread.

TEST YOURSELF
A. There's no point in trying to procrastinate/prevaricate. The store's security man saw you slipping that watch into your pocket.
B. After years of procrastinating/prevaricating Sally and James decided to get married.
C. Procrastination/prevarication is the thief of time.

ANSWERS
A. *Prevaricate*   **B.** *Procrastinating*   **C.** *Procrastination*

Usage Tips
[i] If you have a tendency to put off making difficult but important decisions you have fallen victim to *procrastination*. The word comes from the Latin *pro* (forward) plus *cras* (tomorrow).

ℹ️ A person who *prevaricates* tries to conceal the truth by evading a question or in some other way misleading the questioner. The word comes from *pre* (before) plus *varicare* (to stretch, bend or deviate). *Prevarication* is not the same as outright lying but the difference between the two can be paper thin.

principal/principle

When is the correct ending *-pal* and when should it be *-ple?*

TEST YOURSELF

A. The college principle had no principals and was not above dipping into staffroom funds to pay for his petrol.

B. There are a few details to get right, but in principle I approve of the design.

C. We'll have to go back to first principals if we are to have any chance of cracking the new code.

D. The principal objective set out in the budget was to reduce the debt to a manageable size within four years.

ANSWERS

A. Wrong. The sentence should begin: The college *principal* had no *principles* …

B. *In principle* is correct.

C. *First principals* should be *first principles*.

D. *Principal objective* is correct.

Usage Tips

ℹ️ *Principal* means 'first in importance or rank'. Like the word *prince* it comes from the Latin *princeps* (leader, emperor). Think too of the *principal boy* in pantomime.

ℹ️ *Principles* are basic rules and assumptions which set the guidelines for judging conduct.

prone/prostrate/supine/prostate

Lie flat on the floor face down and you will be either *prone* or *prostrate*. Lie on your back and you will be *supine*. The gland that can cause medical problems for men is the *prostate*.

protest

In Britain, demonstrators will protest a*gainst, about* or *at* an unpopular decision by the government. Americans dispense with the prepositions and simply *protest* the decision. Those who worry that the American usage is starting to establish a bridgehead in Britain should perhaps congratulate themselves on the fact that peaceful protests are, for the most part, still allowed in both countries.

quantum leap

In physics, a *quantum leap* (also called a *quantum jump*) occurs when the atoms or molecules within a system move from one energy level to another. The phrase has come into general use to describe any abrupt and significant change. So far, so good, though scientists may not be very enthusiastic about the borrowing. But beware of using the phrase too freely. There is no justification for applying it to changes that are relatively minor.

questionnaire

This word crossed the Channel long enough ago for it to be pronounced the English way, as in *question*, rather than the French way as if it started with *kest*.

quite

British English and American English both agree and differ over what is meant by *quite*. To deal with agreement first, both take it to mean *very, extremely, entirely* or *completely*. It carries this meaning in, for example, *quite soon, quite correct, quite likely, quite full, quite finished, quite hopeless, quite a mess* and *quite helpless*. But they part company when it comes to such phrases as *quite happy, quite nice, quite hopeful, quite good* and *quite tidy*. To a British ear, *quite* is taken to mean *fairly* or *to a limited extent*. Americans tend to hold firm to *very, extremely* or *completely*.

Sometimes, *quite* can mean either *extremely* or *fairly* in both American and British English. If a girl is described as *quite pretty*, a thinker as *quite clever*, or an argument as *quite persuasive* are these full-hearted compliments or are they limited? The context will generally make things clear, and when the phrases are spoken rather than written, tone of voice is a useful guide. If the emphasis falls on *quite,* the force of the attached adjective is reduced. Conversely, if it falls on the adjective there is no doubt that *quite* means *extremely.*

The use of *Quite!* to indicate agreement with and approval of what has just been stated is long established in Britain but rarely encountered in America.

CURIO CORNER

The forty days of quarantine

An oubreak of plague, the Black Death, that began early in the 14th century, is estimated to have killed three quarters of the population of Europe and Asia. Whether that estimate is accurate or not, what is undeniable is that the disease reached Europe on ships that had visited the Eastern Mediterranean, where the two continents meet. The Venetians, who were at the time the greatest traders in the Western world, took the sensible precaution of refusing entry to suspect ships for 40 days, to establish whether or not plague was aboard. The Italian for a period of 40 days is *quarantina,* which gives us the word *quarantine,* though the period of isolation for a human being, an animal or any object suspected of carrying a contagious disease is no longer set at 40 days.

r r r r R r r r r

racket/racquet

In Britain, either spelling is acceptable for the sports item used to strike a ball or shuttlecock, but *racquet* is the more usual. This avoids confusion with the *racket* that means either an irritatingly loud noise or a scheme to take money out of the pockets of gullible people. Americans stick to the spelling *racket* for all meanings.

rarefy

This is the correct spelling – not *rarify*.

rather

Using *rather* usually indicates that a choice has been, is being or has to be made, but sometimes the word can creep into a sentence when it is not needed.

TEST YOURSELF
A. Some music lovers would rather sit in the garden and enjoy the dawn chorus than listen to certain contemporary composers.
B. It may be cheaper and it is certainly safer to pay an expert rather than to tackle some electrical jobs yourself.
C. That drive of John's on the last hole was rather spectacular.
D. Nobody wants to work for a boss who is quicker to pick out faults rather than to give praise for a job well done.
E. There's not much on TV tonight, so why don't we rather go for a walk?

ANSWERS
A. Correct.
B. Incorrect. Delete *rather*.
C. Correct.
D. Incorrect. Delete *rather*.
E. Incorrect – except in some African countries.

Usage Tips

ⓘ When *than* on its own can carry the full meaning of *rather than*, as in Sentences **B** and **D**, the word *rather* is redundant.

ⓘ The typically British habit of using *rather* to add emphasis to the expression of an opinion, as in Sentence **C**, should be practised with care. It is not acceptable when the word it modifies conveys the idea of something pushed to an extreme. A golf shot may be *rather spectacular* but it cannot be *rather outstanding*. A robbery may be *rather daring* but it cannot be *rather outrageous*. And nothing can be described as *rather unique*.

ⓘ The way *rather* is used in Sentence **D** is acceptable in South Africa and in some other African countries, but is not approved elsewhere. Say either *why don't we go for a walk instead?* or *would you rather go for a walk instead?*

re

When reading legal documents and formal business letters it can be reassuring to come across *re*, meaning 'with reference to'. It means you are dealing with professionals. But *re* sounds stiff to the point of being arthritic when it is used outside the world of lawyers, bankers and businesspeople. A job application that begins, 'Re your advertisement…' is more likely to end up in the wastepaper basket than on the short list.

reason

When *reason* is used as a noun there is a strong temptation to tag on such words as *why, because, owing to* and *on account of*. The temptation should be resisted.

TEST YOURSELF

A. The reason why John turned down the central heating was because he was staggered by the size of his bill for the last quarter.

B. The reason I am poking down the back of the sofa is that I have a strong feeling my missing specs might be there.

C. 'Theirs not to reason why/Theirs but to do and die' (Alfred, Lord Tennyson).

D. There are several reasons why I think we are unlikely to win the tennis grand slam this year, and the first is that our players are not hungry enough.

E. The only reason why Geraldine agreed to stay longer was because the rain was bucketing down and she had no umbrella.

G. Bankers claim that the reason why some of them are awarded huge bonuses is because otherwise they might take their talents elsewhere.

ANSWERS

A. Delete *why* or substitute *that*.

B. Correct.

C. Correct. Tennyson is using *reason* as a verb.

D. The *why* in this case is acceptable to all but die-in-the-last-ditch purists.

E. Delete *why* and substitute *that* for *because*.

G. Delete *why* and substitute *that* for *because*.

Usage Tips

ℹ️ Although *the reason is because* may be found in the work of writers as revered as P. G. Wodehouse, this construction is not accepted as standard English. Other phrases condemned to join it in the reject bin are *The reason is due to/owing to/on account of*.

To be sure of using standard English either leave out such words altogether or say *the reason that.*

ℹ️ A handful of hyper-careful speakers would also ban *the reason why.* They would either drop *why* or replace it with *that* or *for.* But this use of *why* has become well established and is widely acceptable. In a few instances, as in Sentence **D**, it is difficult to see how *why* might be avoided without making it necessary to re-cast the entire sentence.

ℹ️ When *reason* is used as a verb, as in Tennyson's poem *The Charge of the Light Brigade,* there is no possible objection to coupling *reason* with *why.*

rebound/redound

The first means 'to bounce back', often in a harmful way. The second means 'to have an effect', often in a beneficial way. An action or statement, usually made with ill intentions, may *rebound* on the reputation of the person responsible for it – as in *If you persist in saying I was telling lies it will only rebound on you.* When an action or a statement could be beneficial, *redound* is more appropriate – as in *If you will take the blame openly and honestly it can only redound to your credit.*

recognise

It is distressingly common, in more than one sense of the word, to pronounce this word *rekernise,* without sounding the *g.*

Red Indian

This term is regarded as offensive. Say *Native American* instead.

refer back

Guardians of style have a point when they say that far too often *back* is added to *refer* when it is not needed.

TEST YOURSELF

A. A heckler rose to her feet and referred the MP back to a speech in which, only a few months ago, what he said was exactly opposite to what he was saying now.

B. May I refer you back to what George Orwell had to say on this very subject?

C. Councillor Shufflebottom proposed that the decision on whether or not to install traffic lights at the junction should be referred back to the Highways Committee.

ANSWERS

A. Delete *back*.

B. Delete *back*.

C. *Back* is correct if the Highways Committee is being asked to reconsider a previous decision about the traffic lights, but delete *back* if this is the first time their decision has been requested.

Usage Tip

ℹ️ Warning lights should flash if ever you are tempted to say or write *refer back*, because *back* is usually superfluous. The only time it is acceptable is when, as in Sentence **C**, the matter in hand has already been referred to, and a second reference is called for.

CURIO CORNER

Dr Johnson refutes a theory

A useful distinction is in danger of being lost as more and more people use *refute* as if it meant exactly the same as *deny*. Careful speakers use *refute* only when the denial is supported by convincing proof. Dr Johnson, renowned for his wit, good sense and mastery of words, was once asked by his biographer and friend James Boswell how he would refute the proposition that objects in the world around us have no independent existence outside the human imagination. He kicked a stone and declared: 'I refute it thus!' Nobody denies that the language has moved on since Dr Johnson's time, and some authorities maintain that the distinction between the two words is no longer valid. But it would be a sad loss to the language if *refute* were to lose its special meaning.

regard

It is acceptable English though rather stiff and official-sounding to say or write *with regard to*. The phrase is better kept for business letters, legal documents and the like. What is never acceptable is to make the noun plural and say *with regards to*.

relations/relatives

There is no justification for the belief that *relatives* is somehow a more respectful word than *relations*. When applied to people who are related by blood or marriage these two words are all but completely interchangeable. The only instances when this is not so are when referring to *elderly relatives* and to either *rich relations* or *poor relations*.

research

The American pronunciation for the noun – **re**search, with the accent on the first syllable – has begun to make inroads in Britain but is not accepted by careful speakers. For them, the stress for both the verb and the noun falls on the second syllable – re**search** – and it is likely to remain there.

respectively

There are occasions when this word is needed in order to avoid confusion. For example, the statement *John and Mary excelled at Maths and English* could mean either that both were high achievers in both subjects or that John was outstanding in Maths and Mary in English. Adding *respectively* would make it clear that the second meaning was intended. Some over-cautious writers, however, tend to use the word more often than is necessary. It is not needed, for instance, in such a sentence as *John and Mary started at nursery school at ages three and four respectively*. When the context already makes the meaning clear, all that *respectively* does is to cause a slight but unnecessary delay in comprehension.

restauranteur

There is no such word. A *restaurant*, a word borrowed from France, is a place where energy and feelings of well-being are restored by good food, good wine and good company. The proprietor of a restaurant is someone who restores – hence a *restaurateur*.

result

A football team that loses 5–0 has still obtained a *result*, although that is not the word its manager would be likely to use. A loss or a draw is a *result*, just as surely as a win. But in the world of sport the word has come to mean only one thing. Kevin Keegan, when he was the manager of Newcastle United, told a radio interviewer: 'The team know what we have to do to get a few results.' Yes, Kevin, but to get them, all your team needs to do is to turn up. The idea that a result and a win are the same thing probably spills over from the language of crime fighting. When the police say they have won a result this means a crime has been solved and the perpetrator caught.

Reverend

Tradition in the Anglican Church dictates that the title *The Reverend* should be followed by a Christian name or initials and not just by the surname alone. In High Church circles throughout the English-speaking world the preferred form of address is *The Reverend Martin Robinson* or *The Reverend M. Robinson* rather than *The Reverend Robinson*. However, omitting the Christian name is becoming acceptable in many places as standard English. This is especially the case in America, though with some notable exceptions. Tradition carries the day when referring to *The Reverend Jesse Jackson* or *The Reverend Martin Luther King*. It is acceptable when giving the full title to abbreviate *The Reverend* to *The Rev.* but it is regarded as lacking in respect to refer to a clergyman or clergywoman as simply *The Rev.*

riband/ribbon

Between the wars there was no distinction prized more highly by the captains of the *Queen Mary*, the *Normandie* and other great ocean liners than for their ship to be awarded the *blue riband*. It meant that their floating luxury hotel had crossed the North Atlantic faster than any of its competitors. Even today the phrase is occasionally used as a mark of excellence, but otherwise it has been superseded by the similar-sounding *blue ribbon*.

right/rightly

It is not always easy to make the right choice between these two words, but knowing some general principles will help.

TEST YOURSELF
A. Alice was quite right to ask for some identification before she opened the door.
B. Alice asked, quite rightly, for some identification before she opened the door.
C. If I remember right/rightly, we have already met – on holiday in Spain, three years ago.
D. Stop playing with the dog and get back to your homework right this minute.
E. Mother will be right glad to see you.
F. Turn left at the lights, go past the school and the house you are looking for is right/just there, in front of your eyes.

ANSWERS
A. Correct.
B. Correct.
C. Either word is acceptable, with *rightly* sounding slightly more formal.
D. Correct.
E. See usage tips below.
F. Either word is acceptable.

Usage Tips
ℹ️ When the American way of using *right* to mean 'at once, straight away' first came to Britain it met a cold reception from careful speakers. They saw it as being informal at best. But the usage

had staying power and is now accepted as standard English on both sides of the Atlantic.

[i] Similarly, using *right* as in Sentence **E**, to mean 'just, exactly' was once regarded as informal but is now accepted as standard English.

[i] Using *right* as an intensifier, to mean 'extremely, very, exceptionally', as in Sentence **E**, was once standard English. This usage is now, with a few exceptions, encountered only in regional dialects. The exceptions include its use in titles such as Right Honourable.

rob

The difference between *rob* and *steal* ought to be clear. A person or a place is *robbed*, and illicitly acquired cash is *stolen*. Thieves *rob* a bank and *steal* the money or *rob* a church and *steal* the lead off its roof. But it is increasingly common for *robbing* to take over from *stealing*. Characters in a film or on television might say *We went out twice a week robbing lead* or *I'm going to rob steel at the old factory*. This is not standard English and there is no justification for blurring a useful distinction.

robbery

The difference between *robbery* and *theft* is that for *robbery* to be the charge the theft must involve violence or the threat of violence. See also **burglary**.

rubbish

To dismiss an opponent's arguments as *rubbish* may not be very polite but it is standard English. To treat the noun as if it were a verb and *rubbish* an opponent or an argument is, at least for the present, so informal as to be not far from slang.

S s S § ⠇S⠇ *S* **s** *s* **s** S

salutary

This word is often mis-spelled as *salutory*.

same

The use of *the same* in place of *it* or *them* is best confined to legal documents and extremely formal business letters. *The search documents have finally arrived and I will, as promised, send you copies of the same* is well enough when buying or selling a house but such language would look strange in a letter to a friend.

sank/sunk

Should you say *the ship sank* or *the ship sunk*? In standard English, *sank* is the correct past tense of *sink* if the verb is active while *sunk* is the right choice if the verb is passive, as in *the ship was sunk*. Increasingly, however, *sunk* is being used when the verb is active, as in *the ship sunk*. This usage has been accepted by some authorities in America but in Britain and other parts of the English-speaking world it is regarded as informal.

sat/sitting/seated

It is becoming distressingly common to hear *I was sat* instead of *I was sitting*.

TEST YOURSELF
A. David was in his usual place – sat on a park bench and feeding the ducks.

B. Since she was the guest of honour, Kate was seated at the right hand of the host.

C. I was sat on a park bench, minding my own business and feeding the ducks, when who should come along but a friend I hadn't seen in years.

ANSWERS

A. Incorrect. Say *sitting*, not *sat*.

B. Correct.

C. Incorrect. Say *was sitting*, not *was sat*.

Usage Tip

ℹ️ The past tense of the phrase *I sit* can be either *I sat* or *I was sitting*. *I was sat* is the passive form of the verb, which should be used only when somebody has taken a decision for you and allocated you to a particular seat.

scarify

This word may sound like a combination of *scare* and *terrify* but it has nothing to do with either. It means 'to scratch' or 'to scar'. A gardener who *scarifies* the lawn is not trying to frighten worms but to get rid of moss.

schedule

'Where on earth,' the Englishman asked the American, 'did you learn to pronounce this word *skedule* instead of *shedule*?' The reply: 'In school.'

scone

Pronounced *skon*, not *skoan*, unless you are aspiring to sound genteel.

Scots, Scottish, Scotch

To put the matter simply, the first is a person, the second an adjective and the third a drink. In practice the choice is not quite so simple. The rule is followed in references to *Mary, Queen of Scots* and in the theatrical tradition of warding off bad luck by saying *The Scottish Play*, rather than *Macbeth*. Convention dictates referring both to the *Scottish Parliament* and to a *Scottish regiment* as well as to the *Scots Guards*, *Scotch eggs*, the *Scotch-Irish* and *Scotch mist*. In Canada and America it is acceptable to use *Scotch* as the adjective of choice, whatever the noun it is attached to.

sea change/step change

Why must every change, other than the most minor, be described as a *sea change* or a *step change*? The metaphors have been drained of their impact through over-use. Politicians in particular tend to be fonder of announcing *sea changes* and *step changes* than they should be. For most of us, *major changes* are impressive enough.

sensual/sensuous

Both words relate to pleasure that is derived from the physical senses, and they are sometimes interchangeable, but they can also point in different directions.

TEST YOURSELF
A. Charles Lamb described the sensuous/sensual delight he took in old china as being 'almost feminine'.
B. Muriel sank to the floor and stretched sensuously/sensually.
C. The officer in charge of censoring letters from troops at the front disliked his job intensely because he was easily embarrassed by their sensuous/sensual content.
D. Ian Fleming endowed 007 James Bond with looks that were both commanding and sensuous/sensual.

ANSWERS
A. *Sensuous.*
B. Either word could be appropriate.
C. *Sensual.*
D. *Sensual.*

Usage Tip

ℹ️ *Sensuous* is the word for delights that are intellectual and aesthetic, while *sensual* carries the notion of pleasures that are sexual.

sexist language

There is no question that before feminism hit its stride, in the 1970s, the language was male-dominated. Words and phrases that are now clearly seen to diminish the status of women were once used without much thought. The main battle for language equality has been won but there are still some mopping up operations to be completed. How would you avoid sexist language in the following sentences?

TEST YOURSELF

A. The air hostess gave us a dazzling smile when she brought round the drinks trolley.

B. My charlady not only keeps the house clean and tidy – she even helps with the ironing.

C. After a moment or two's harrumping to clear his throat, the chairman called the meeting to order.

D. Four fully manned engines were sent to tackle the blaze, but the firemen still took hours to bring it under control.

E. 'No man is an Island, entire of itself' (John Donne).

F. A company spokesman discounted rumours that the firm was heading for financial meltdown, but then he would say that, wouldn't he?

G. The authoress Jane Austen showed a fine perception of human foibles in every character she created.

H. No matter how many man-hours it took to build their Great Wall, the Chinese seem never to have suffered from a shortage of manpower.

I. With the price of metal shooting to the sky, thieves are beginning to steal manhole covers.

ANSWERS

Some of the answers below go beyond changing a single word and call for a sentence to be partly or totally recast.

A. Say *steward* instead of *air hostess*.

B. Say *cleaner* or *home help* instead of *charlady*. Avoid *she* by substituting *and*.

C. *Chair* and *chairperson* are gender-neutral words, though there are still traditionalists who cannot bring themselves to use these terms, and prefer *chairman* or *chairwoman*, whichever is appropriate. To get rid of *clearing his throat*, say *and throat clearing*.

D. Say *firefighters* instead of *firemen*, and *fully crewed* instead of *fully manned*.

E. This is a line by one of our greatest poets, so leave it alone.

F. Say *spokesperson* instead of *spokesman*, and rephrase the ending of the sentence to read *but that's exactly what somebody in that job would say, isn't it?*

G. Say *author* or *novelist* – not *authoress*.

H. You could say *a shortage of labour* instead of *a shortage of manpower*, but this reduces the force of the expression. Sometimes, as with *manpower* and *man-hours*, there is no alternative that is fully acceptable. *Person-power* and *person-hours* are risible. Perhaps the best solution, if no elegant way of rephrasing comes to mind, would be to grit your teeth and be content with manpower and man-hours.

I. See **Curio Corner** below.

Usage Tip

ℹ️ Be on guard against using words carrying the assumption that managerial and other important jobs can be filled only by men, or that only men have the natural authority to take charge. Being of the 'wrong' gender once barred the way to a number of professions and careers. A doctor or a lawyer could only be a man, and nurses were almost always female. Today, doctor and lawyer have become gender-neutral terms and many hospital wards have male as well as female nurses. Tagging *-ess* on to a word, as in *authoress, sculptress* and *poetess*, is usually seen as diminishing to women – and rightly so. But there are exceptions. Nobody is likely to turn down an Oscar for *Best Actress*. Nor are the words *princess, duchess* and *heiress* likely to cause offence. *Governess* is a special case, for it is not the female of *governor*. A *governess* in, say a Brontë novel, is a woman who is paid to educate and bring up a rich man's children. The *governor* of a prison, or of an American State can be either a man or a woman.

CURIO CORNER

The swing of the pendulum

It would take a bold man to go into a crowded pub and call for a *ploughperson's lunch*. Yet this has been seriously suggested as the politically correct term for a simple pub meal. Along with attempts to abolish such terms as *fisherman, masterpiece, mastermind and master bedroom* this raises the question of whether the pendulum has, in some cases, swung back too far. Extreme feminists have even declared war on a syllable, suggesting that *manhole covers* should be changed to *maintenance covers*. The old joke that Man embraces Woman no longer raises many laughs, and there is a sound case for saying *humankind* or *humanity* instead of *mankind*. But the biblical pronouncement *Man shall not live by bread alone* was never meant to apply only to the male gender.

shall/will

An old and not very funny joke tells of a man who, when he fell into a river, called out in despair: 'Oh! I will drown, I will drown and nobody shall save me!' The bystanders did nothing because they believed that 'I will' meant he wanted to drown and 'nobody shall' was simply his prediction of what would happen. In fact, the joke is on those who believe that *I/we shall* is always the correct usage when dealing with the simple future and *I/we will* implies a deliberate intention, even determination, to make something happen. The choice between *shall* and *will* is governed not by hard-and-fast rules but by a set of conventions that are subject to change. See also **should/would**.

TEST YOURSELF

A. They shall/will not pass.
B. Shall/will you have a drink now or shall/will we dance?
C. 'We shall/will fight on the beaches, we shall/will fight on the landing grounds… we shall/will fight in the hills; we shall/will never surrender' (Winston Churchill).
D. When shall/will I see you again?
E. 'Shall/will I compare thee to a summer's day?' (Shakespeare).
F. 'I shall/will arise and go now, and go to Innisfree' (W. B. Yeats).
G. 'That'll be the day, when we say goodbye' (Buddy Holly song).
H. Come out of that puddle when you're wearing new shoes. I won't/shan't tell you again.

ANSWERS
A. *Shall*.
B. *Will* and *shall*.
C. *Shall*.
D. Either word could be appropriate.
E. *Shall*.
F. *Will*.
G. *That'll* is informal but is often used as the contracted form of both *that shall* and, as in Sentence **G**, of *that will*.
H. Either word is acceptable to speakers of British English, but *won't* would be the only choice for an American. The contraction *shan't* is not used in American English.

Usage Tips

ℹ️ The traditional default position was that *I/we shall* was used for the simple future, whereas *I/we will* expressed intention, or determination about a desired result. Conversely, *will* indicated the simple future and *shall* a deliberate intention when used with non-first person pronouns such as *you, he, she, we* and *it*.

ℹ️ However much it may be deplored by traditionalists, *shall* is on the retreat throughout the English-speaking world, and *will* is taking over as a standard way of indicating the future. The only stout rearguard action against this development is in England itself. This may be because of the pull of tradition. Winston Churchill used *shall* in one of his most stirring wartime speeches (Sentence **C**) and Shakespeare used *shall* in one of his greatest sonnets (Sentence **F**).

ℹ️ *Shall* also survives when questions are put in the first person (I/ we) – as in Sentence **D**.

ℹ️ One way of avoiding the possibility of making the wrong choice is to abbreviate *shall* or *will* to *'ll*, as in Sentence **G**. This, however, is informal. Another way is to rephrase and say something like *I plan to…* or *I am going to…*

should/would

Just as *shall* is being replaced by *will* so, at a slower rate, is *should* beginning to be pushed aside by *would*. There are still, however, occasions when only one of them is appropriate. *Should* is often the better choice if you wish to imply that something is required or that the person addressed has a duty to act. See also **shall/will**.

TEST YOURSELF

A. If I were you I would/should keep that dog on a chain, and a short one too.

B. John had an uneasy feeling that he would/should think twice before signing the document.

C. Very few of those who have visited Seoul on duty would/should care to go there for a holiday.

D. If Jenny had not shortened her stride before the last hurdle she would/should probably have been the winner.

E. I would/should like to propose a toast to the bridesmaids.

F. Thank you for the offer, but I wouldn't/shouldn't dream of taking the last chocolate in the box.

G. What I have to say is important but wouldn't/shouldn't take long.

H. What would/should we do if we can't find the key?

I. Martin had hidden our keys as a practical joke. What would/should he do next?

J. 'He would/should, wouldn't/shouldn't he?'

K. It's very hot in here. Shall/should I open a window?

ANSWERS

A. *Would.*

B. *Should.*

C. *Would.*

D. *Would.*

E. Either word would be appropriate, with *should* sounding a shade more polite.

F. *Wouldn't.*

G. *Shouldn't.*

H. *Should.*

I. *Would.*

J. *Would* and *wouldn't.*

K. Both words are acceptable in British English, with *shall* ahead by a nose. In the United States, the speaker would say *Should I open the window?* and in parts of Ireland *Will I open the window?*

Usage Tip

ℹ️ Just as *will* is taking over from *shall,* so *would* is beginning to push aside *should* – to the dismay of traditionalists. This process has gone farther in America than in Britain, though in both countries it is far from complete. If the idea to be conveyed is that something *ought to* happen, as in Sentence **B**, the word to choose is *should.* This applies also if, as in Sentences **G** and **H**, it is inevitable – at least highly likely – that something will happen.

ℹ️ *Would* can express a preference, as in Sentence **F**, or a possibility, as in Sentence **D**.

ℹ️ The contractions *would've* and *should've* are acceptable though informal. The contractions *would of* and *should of* are never acceptable. These two howlers probably arose because the offending *of* sounds close to *'ve.*

ℹ️ Another howler, encountered in American slang, is the way *should* is misused in such statements as *I want you should be there on time*. This probably arose because America is a melting pot of languages as well as of peoples.

silicon/silicone

Silicon, the main ingredient of sand, is one of the most common elements on the planet. The silicon chip is used in transistors – hence Silicon Valley, which is the heart of the computer industry. *Silicone* is a plastic that contains not only silicon but also oxygen, carbon and hydrogen. It is used in the space industry, in nonstick frying pans and for making artificial limbs.

situation

This has now become a vogue word, and those who trot it out thoughtlessly are much mocked. It is advisable to avoid such phrases as *a winner takes all situation, a love on the dole situation* or *a learning curve situation*. Even when it is used appropriately – as in *a desperate situation, an unhappy situation* or *a vacant situation* – some taint from its misuse may still linger on. Often the word can be avoided altogether but, if not, at least it should be used sparingly.

sledge, sled, sleigh

Most Britons use the word they grew up with – *sledge*. But the North American *sled* and *sleigh* are making inroads. The Winter Olympics sport is *bobsleigh,* Americans and Canadians go on *sleigh rides* and it would be difficult to think of a Russian, pursued by wolves across the frozen wastes of Siberia, as riding on anything other than a *sleigh*.

something

It is common to hear this word pronounced as if it rhymes with *think*, rather than with *thing*. This error is not to be encouraged. See also **anything**.

split infinitive

The infinitive of a verb – *to go, to laugh, to attempt, to drive, to run* and so on – is its basic form. And one of the most closely policed 'rules' of grammar is that the infinitive should never be split. The opening sequences of the television series *Star Trek* have often been ridiculed because they announce the mission of the space ship *Enterprise* as being *to boldly go where no man has gone before*. Those who argue against splitting the *to* and the rest of the verb base their case on Latin. In Ancient Rome it was impossible to split infinitives because Latin verbs are single words, without a separate *to* to their name. But we speak English, not Latin, and there are times when splitting an infinitive is not only possible but, for the sake of elegance and directness, necessary. Which of the following sentences do you find acceptable, and which would you reject?

TEST YOURSELF
A. Christopher is not likely to openly admit that he ate all the pies.
B. This habit of yours of claiming all the credit and dodging all the blame is beginning to seriously affect our friendship.
C. Michael decided to, whatever the consequences might be, turn down the offer of a new job.
D. Would it be in order to frankly state that I'm not impressed by the cook?
E. Little Johnny tried hard to always hand in his homework on time.
F. Martha had intended to temporarily stay with friends but found herself still living with them after two years.

ANSWERS

Sentences **A** and **B**: Splitting the infinitive sounds natural and is fully acceptable.

Sentence **C**: Reword to read *Michael decided, whatever the consequences might be, to turn down the offer of a new job.*

Sentence **D**: To frankly state is acceptable, but *to state frankly* is better and will not annoy traditionalists.

Sentence **E**: Move *always* so that it comes before *tried hard*.

Sentence **F**: Move *temporarily* so that it comes after *stay*.

Usage Tip

ℹ️ Avoid splitting infinitives whenever you can, but if this makes for an inelegant or unnatural-sounding sentence, take no notice of those who say this is an inflexible rule, and do not hesitate to split when you must.

stalactite/stalagmite

It is easy to remember which is which. *Stalactite* contains a *c*, and is formed from deposits that drip down from the *ceiling* of a cave, while *stalagmite* contains a *g* and is built up from the *ground*.

stationary/stationery

If a train is motionless it is *stationary*. If you need some envelopes, a writing pad and a pen you will need to buy some *stationery*.

step change *See* sea change

storeys/stories

In Britain and in countries that follow British style, a house with more than one floor has two or more *storeys*. In America the word is spelled *stories* and the singular is *story*, not *storey*. There is no agreement either about assigning numbers to different levels. In Britain, the *first floor* is the one immediately above the ground floor, but in America the *first floor* means the ground floor. The seventh floor of a department store in New York would be called the sixth floor in London.

straight/strait

There is a marked difference in meaning between these two sounda-likes – marked but not always observed. A *straight* line is one without curves, and a *straight* answer is one that makes no attempt to dodge the question. A *strait* is a narrow passage between two larger bodies of water – the *Strait of Magellan* for instance, between the Atlantic and the Pacific at the tip of South America. Somebody whose income falls low will be in *straitened circumstances* or even in *dire straits*. A dangerous prisoner or patient might, for safety's sake, be put into a *straitjacket*. So often are the two words confused that some dictionary compilers have come to accept *straightjacket* as an alternative spelling. Careful speakers hold on determinedly to the idea that different meanings call for different spellings.

subjunctive mood

In the sentence 'I overslept because I was at a riotous party last night' the verb *was* is in what is called the indicative mood. In the sentence 'If I were you I would stay away from parties like that if you want to keep your job' the verb *were* is in the subjunctive mood. The indicative is used for statements of fact and deals with things that happen, have happened or will happen. The subjunctive deals with a parallel world in which desired things might happen. In which of the following sentences would you use the subjunctive?

TEST YOURSELF

A. 'If you were the only girl in the world, and I was/were the only boy' (popular song).

B. These demands will benefit all of us, and it is essential that your signature is/be added.

C. Put my name to a set of demands like these? Heaven forbid!

D. If it was/were only a matter of what suited me I might do as you ask.

E. 'If I was/were a blackbird I'd whistle and sing' (popular song).

F. I wish Bryan was/were more like his brother, for then I know he'd be more likely to see things my way.

G. This is a busy junction and safety regulations require that a driver slows/slow down when approaching it.

ANSWERS

A. *Were.*

B. *Be.* In Britain *is* would be acceptable though regarded as informal.

C. *Heaven forbid* is a stock phrase which always takes the subjunctive.

D. *Were*. In Britain, *was* would just about scrape in as the informal choice.

E. *Were*.

F. *Were,* but in British English *was* is acceptable informal usage.

G. *Slow* is grammatically correct but in Britain *slows* would also be widely acceptable.

Usage Tips

ℹ️ Use the subjunctive to express the idea that, if circumstances could be changed, things that are desired, doubtful, unlikely or seemingly impossible might come about.

ℹ️ The words *if*, *wish* and *though* are clues that the subjunctive mood may be appropriate.

ℹ️ The subjunctive is used somewhat hesitantly in Britain, even when good grammar may call for it. In other English-speaking countries, and especially in America, it is used far more readily.

ℹ️ The subjunctive is embodied in a number of stock phrases – among them *be that as it may*, *far be it from me*, *heaven forfend* and *heaven forbid*.

ℹ️ If you feel that the subjunctive is giving an unwanted archaic flavour to what you say or write, it is sometimes possible to avoid it by rephrasing. Sentence **G**, for example, might read … *safety regulations require a driver to slow down*.

supersede

Note that this word is spelled with an *s* in the middle, not a *c*.

sure (that's for sure)

When something is *certain, beyond doubt, totally convincing* or *definitely true* it is in almost all cases advisable to use such words rather than to fall back on *that's for sure*. This comparative newcomer to English's stock of phrases is at best colloquial.

T

tablespoonful/teaspoonful

The plurals are *tablespoonfuls* and *teaspoonfuls*. The terms *tablespoonsful* and *teaspoonsful*, though logical, fell out of use years ago.

take

A recent extension of the meaning of *take* is proving its usefulness practically every day. 'What's your take on yesterday's developments in the Middle East?' an interviewer will ask. This is a quick and clear way of asking a number of questions: 'What in your opinion caused the developments, what do you think will be their likely outcome and what should we do about it?' One word of caution, though: the usage is so young that it has not yet been promoted to the ranks of formal language.

target

Shoot an arrow at a target and your intention is to hit it – a bullseye if you can but, if not, as near to one as possible. Overshooting the target is just as much a miss as falling short. Yet it is not uncommon to hear people awarding themselves points for overreaching a target. The spokesman for a major water company, defending his firm's record on dealing with leaks, said in a radio interview: 'We have hit most of our targets and exceeded some of them.' Some spokesman!

teaspoonful *See* tablespoonful

texting

Love it or loathe it, text messaging is here to stay. And the mobile phone is not entirely to blame.

The first text message predates the world wide web. It was probably born when a lovelorn suitor posted an X to his girlfriend, meaning a kiss. The habit progressed to writing SWALK (Sealed With A Loving Kiss) on an envelope enclosing a love letter. Sometimes a loved one would be reminded that a kiss was BOLTOP (Better On Lips Than On Paper). And the radio comedian Tommy Handley had people bidding each other TTFN (Ta-Ta For Now).

More sophisticated texters developed SMS, the Short Message Service, which originated with radio telegraphy. It spread to the Middle East and Asia, where it also known as TMS (Text Messaging Service).

These systems have now been hijacked – and expanded – by users of mobile phones and emails across the globe. Textspeak is prized by youngsters as their own kind of secret language, meant to exclude parents and other interfering adults.

Even Shakespeare has failed to escape the mutilation of the textspeakers. A student won a Northumbria University award for translating Romeo and Juliet into this new language. The judges found it AOK to write: 'O rmo rmo were4 art thou rmo?' Many will still prefer to read: 'Oh Romeo, Romeo, wherefore art thou Romeo?' Others, however, will still choose 2 txt rather than not2txt.

Textspeak depends heavily on acronyms and vowels are often omitted, with no loss to the understanding, just as they are in Arabic and in shorthand. The derivations of many have become obscure. If in doubt, ask your children!

All 26 letters of the English alphabet and the first ten numerals are used – with a few special symbols thrown in. The texter sends the texts and the textee, reluctantly or otherwise, receives them.

This new language is rapidly becoming the biz in commerce and the preferred means of communicating between m8s (mates).

The following may answer some of your ?s (questions) and provide a grounding for understanding this strange new language:

?4U	I have a question for you
@TEOTD	At the end of the day
143	I love you (Three little words, with one, four and three letters)
1432	I love you too
182	I hate you
10X	Thanks
1CE	Once
2G2BT	Too good to be true
2MOR	Tomorrow
2NTE	Tonight
2MI	Too much information
459	I love you (459 is ILY on the keypad)
6Y	Sexy
7Y	Sick
88	Hugs and kisses
9	Parent is watching
A3	Anywhere, anytime, any place
ADBB	All done, bye-bye
AMBW	All my best wishes
BTW	Back to work
B9	Boss is watching
BAU	Business as usual
BFF	Best friends forever
C&G	Chuckle and grin
CB	Coffee break
CID	Consider it done
CYO	See you online
DGT	Don't go there
DYJKHIW	Don't you just hate it when

DYOR	Do your own research
E1	Everyone
E123	Easy as one, two, three
EMA	Email address
EWI	Emailing while intoxicated
F2F	Face to face
FB	Facebook
FOMCL	Fall off my chair laughing
G2CU	Good to see you
G4C	Gone for coffee
GTG	Got to go
HAG1	Have a good one
HRU	How are you
HTH	Hope this helps
IA8	I already ate
IAAA	I am an accountant
IMO	In my opinion
JJ	Just joking
JT	Just teasing
JTLK	Just to let you know
KOC	Kiss on cheek
KEWL	Cool
KUYGW	Keep up the good work
LHO	Laughing head off
LMIRL	Let's meet in real life
LMK	Let me know
LOL	Laugh Out Loud (Not, if you wish to be totally with it, Lots Of Love)
M8	Mate
MGMT	Management
MNC	Mother Nature calls
nOOb	Newbie

N1	No one
NFM	Not for me
O4U	Only for you
OATUS	On a totally unrelated subject
OH	Overheard
PAW	Parent watching
PCM	Please call me
PROGGY	Computer program
QC	Quality control
QFU	Question for you
QTPI	Cutie Pie
R	Are
R8	Rate
RX	Regards
S2S	Sorry to say
SH	Same here
SIMYC	Sorry I missed your call
T+	Positive
TARFU	Things are really fouled up
TYVM	Thank you very much
UGTBK	You've got to be kidding
URSKTM	You are so kind to me
UL	Upload
VFM	Value for money
VGC	Very good condition
VM	Voicemail
W@	What
W/B	Welcome back
WDYK	What do you know
XME	Excuse me
XLNT	Excellent
XLR8	Accelerate, get a move on

YBS	You'll be sorry
Y2K	You're too kind
YWSYLS	You win some, you lose some
Z	Zero
Z	Said
ZZZZZZ	I'm bored

tire/tyre

A British driver will ask for his car to be fitted with new *tyres*. An American motorist will ask for new *tires*.

CURIO CORNER

Where were the Titanic's deck chairs?

When a Cabinet Minister or anybody else in high office responds to a crisis by hurrying to making changes that seem to amount to little more than window-dressing, opponents think they are making a telling point if they compare all the ineffective fuss to *rearranging the deck chairs on the Titanic*. But it was close to midnight on 14 April 1912 when an iceberg ripped open the ship's hull below the waterline. The sea temperature was –2° C (28°F) and it is hardly likely that deck chairs would have been set out in the middle of the night in such freezing conditions. They would have been neatly stacked away, making a nonsense of the deck chairs metaphor.

---

tortuous/torturous

A road that winds and twists the way to its destination or a legal dispute beset by seemingly endless complications is *tortuous*. The word comes from the Latin *tortus* (a twist). An experience that causes severe discomfort or pain – an aching tooth that keeps you awake all night, or being involved in a bitter dispute with a neighbour – is *torturous*, a word that comes from the same root as *torture*.

toward/towards

In countries where British English holds sway, this word almost always has an *s* at the end: *towards*. In the United States, Canada and other lands where American English is spoken, it is almost always *toward*.

trait

Words borrowed from France can take some time to fully embed themselves in the language, and traditionalists insist that there is only one correct pronunciation of *trait*: tray. But 'trayt' is heard so often that it is on the verge of being fully accepted in Britain – as has long been the case in America.

transport/transportation

There used to be a generally accepted distinction between these two words in Britain. *Transport* meant moving goods or people from one place to another, while *transportation* meant sending convicts to the colonies. The distinction has been blurred, but is doggedly upheld by traditionalists. They regard *transportation,* when used to indicate the conveyance of goods and people, as an intrusive Americanism.

Trooping the Colour

The ceremony of *Trooping the Colour,* held on the second Saturday in June, on Horse Guards Parade, Whitehall, to mark the official birthday of the British monarch, is sometimes erroneously referred to as *The Trooping of the Colour.*

try and/try to

Attempts to establish a clear distinction between *try to* and *try and* have met with only partial success. Choosing between the two is often more a matter of instinct and convention than of applying an inflexible rule.

TEST YOURSELF

A. No matter how unimportant a job may seem, Helen always tries to do/tries and does her best.

B. This is the third time I've been unable to get that old banger of yours to start, so why don't you try and/try to do it yourself?

C. When Tony had a rare win at the races his closest friends advised him to try and/try to put something aside for a rainy day.

D. Whatever you say I'm going to fix that leak, so don't try and/try to stop me!

E. Why don't we try and/try to write out a list of all the items we are likely to need on a canal holiday?

F. Isn't it time to face up to the fact that you shouldn't, at your age, try and/try to run after buses?

G. Could you try a bit harder and/to remember the password for your internet banking account?

H. Is there time for me to try and/try to finish off the crossword before we sit down to eat?

ANSWERS

A. *Tries to.*

B. Either choice is acceptable, with *tries to* having a slight edge.

C. Both forms are acceptable, with *try and* having a slight edge.

D. *Try to.*

E. *Try to.*

F. *Try to.*

G. *Try … to.*

H. *Try and.*

Usage Tips

ⓘ If what is being attempted is likely to be achieved, as in Sentences **C** and **H**, *try and* is often more suitable than *try to*.

ⓘ *Try to* is a shade or two more formal than *try and*, so it is usually the better choice if you are in any doubt about which to use. However…

i If, as in Sentence **B**, the word *to* has already been used in a sentence it is often preferable to avoid repetition and use *try and*.

i If what is being attempted is unlikely to happen, as in Sentences **B** and **G**, *try to* is the right choice.

i *Try and*, though more often encountered in British English than American English, is also suitable when, as in Sentence **D**, you are being especially assertive.

Tsar/Czar

Both spellings are acceptable, with *Tsar* more usual in British English and *Czar* in American English.

ɯ u ʊ u̇ U ʋ u u u

U and Non-U

In the mid-1950s a book entitled *Noblesse Oblige* set in motion a game that caused a minor social stir. By identifying some of the speech mannerisms of the upper classes it made them available to those who were less privileged. The author, Nancy Mitford, drew heavily on the research work of Professor Alan C. Ross, inventor of the terms U and Non-U, meaning Upper class and Non-Upper class. A list was compiled of words, phrases and pronunciations that were better avoided. They were frowned upon as being pretentious attempts by the aspiring middle classes to use 'refined' language. Among them were:

Non-U	U
pardon	*what*
mirror	*looking glass*
toilet	*lavatory*
handbag	*bag*
serviette	*napkin*
costly	*dear*
perfume	*scent*
afters/sweet/seconds	*pudding*
settee	*sofa*
lounge	*drawing room/living room*
jacket potatoes	*baked potatoes*
mantlepiece	*chimneypiece*
she's expecting	*she's pregnant*
the wife/my better half	*my wife*

pronouncing *scone* as *scoan*, rather than *skon*
pronouncing *either* as *ee-ther*, rather than eye-ther

Words that came naturally to the upper classes were held to be blunter than the 'genteel' alternatives. Came the Sixties and a reaction began to set in. The Beatles and other pop groups made a Northern accent and a working-class vocabulary not only acceptable but in some contexts almost obligatory. In a kind of inverse snobbery, some speakers tried to pass themselves off as more working class than in fact they were. This trend has continued with the spread of Estuary English and of the fake Cockney accent known as Mockney. As for U and Non-U, a few of the U-words have shown staying power. *Napkin* is one such, and *loo* is usurping the place of both *toilet* and *lavatory*. *Looking glass* and *chimneypiece* survive in stately homes, for instance, but they were never going to catch on among people who see the inside of such places only when they are open to the public. And nobody is likely to lose caste these days for referring to a *handbag*. The tide of U and Non-U has receded, leaving just a few ripples in the sand. Still, it was fun while it lasted.

underestimated/understated/underrated

A mysterious virus has burrowed its way into the language. It chooses for its victims those who would normally be expected to take special care over their words – politicians, speakers on the BBC, columnists who write for serious newspapers and suchlike. Perhaps they are trying too hard to make what they say sound important. The symptom of the virus is that those afflicted say *underestimate, underrated* or *understated* when they mean the exact opposite: *overestimated, overrated* or *overstated*. Fortunately, there is an antidote. Anybody tempted to use such words should simply pause and think first.

TEST YOURSELF

A. 'We cannot underestimate the damage the issue over MPs' expenses has done to the public trust' (Jenny Watson, head of the Electoral Commission).

B. It is impossible to overestimate Constable's impact on landscape painting.

C. 'There remains one special worry for the party, and it cannot be understated' (political columnist).

D. The dangers faced by Captain Cook as he explored the southern oceans ought not to be underestimated.

E. The cost of building a new football stadium compared with that of improving the present one cannot be underestimated.

F. 'I do not think his contribution to snooker can be underestimated. He brought a genius quality that probably hadn't been seen before' (tribute to snooker legend Alex 'Hurricane' Higgins).

ANSWERS

A. Incorrect. Say either *We cannot overestimate* or *We should not underestimate*.

B. Correct.

C. Incorrect. Say either *it should not be understated* or *it cannot be overstated*.

D. Correct.

E. Incorrect. Say either *should not be underestimated* or *cannot be overestimated*.

F. What the tribute-payer meant to say was that Hurricane Higgins's contribution to snooker could not be overestimated.

Usage Tips

ℹ️ To say that something *cannot be underestimated* is awarding it an extremely low estimation – in fact the lowest possible. Yet the phrase is often used, or rather misused, to suggest that no estimation could be too high. If, say, a man's honesty *cannot* be underestimated, then do not trust him with your wallet, for the only logical conclusion is that his honesty *can* be over-estimated.

ℹ️ Whenever you come across the claim that something *cannot* be underestimated it is worth asking yourself whether the speaker really means *should not*. Or, making the same point in a different way, was it the speaker's intention to say *cannot be overestimated*?

[i] Other words that are often misused in the same way as *underestimated* are *understated* and *underrated*.

uninterested *See* disinterested

unique

Purists are quick to stamp on such descriptions as *most unique, very unique* and *almost unique*. Any attempt to establish degrees of uniqueness, they point out, is flying in the face of logic, for every unique thing is the only one of its kind. But does this mean there is a blanket ban on linking any descriptive word with *unique*?

TEST YOURSELF
A. James naïvely believed that no hacker could break into his computer because he never told anybody his own unique password.
B. The jade vase that came up for sale at Sotheby's last week was almost unique.
C. What could be more unique than the endurance and zeal of the Soviet miner Alexei Stakhanov, whose name was to become a byword for productivity?
D. The Atacama desert, parts of which saw no rain in 400 years, is one of the most unique places on earth.
E. The red-necked phalarope is highly unique among British birds because the female initiates courtship and the drably coloured male bird incubates the eggs.

ANSWERS
A. Correct.
B. Correct, although this usage might well be disputed by purists.
C. Incorrect. Say *more remarkable, more extraordinary* or even *more superhuman* instead of *more unique*.
D. Incorrect. Say *most extraordinary, most astonishing* or *most peculiar* instead of *most unique*.
E. Incorrect. Delete *highly,* for it adds nothing to the force of *unique*.

Usage Tips

ℹ️ Since *unique* means 'the only one of its kind', it is a mistake to suggest there is a hierarchy in which some brands of uniqueness are more equal than others. This rules out such descriptions as *very unique, most unique, more unique, highly unique, remarkably unique, somewhat unique, rather unique* and *fairly unique*.

ℹ️ There are, however, some words that indicate not so much a hierarchy as the possibility that some things, while not yet *unique*, are not far from being so. This means that it is perfectly logical to describe something as being *almost unique, nearly unique, practically unique, truly unique, perhaps unique* or *absolutely unique*. Even so, sticklers for tradition disapprove of phrases that suggest something is close to being unique but has not yet achieved the full status.

ℹ️ To be perfectly safe, and avoid upsetting such sticklers, it is worth considering alternatives such as *uncommon, unequalled, outstanding, extremely rare, most remarkable, one of only three left in the world*, and so on.

until

The dictionary definition of *until* is 'up to a stated time', so it is neither necessary nor correct to add the word *up* and say *up until*.

used to

No problems arise when a statement is made that something *used to* be the case. But what is the right way to use this phrase when making a negative statement or asking a question?

TEST YOURSELF
A. You used to be the leading chess player in the club.
B. Did you used to be the leading chess player in the club?
C. Didn't you use to be the leading chess player in the club?
D. Used you not to be the leading table tennis player in the club?
E. You used to be the leading chess player in the club, didn't you?

ANSWERS

A. Correct. This is a simple statement about the way things were.

B. Incorrect.

C. Correct, but it sounds awkward.

D. Correct, but it sounds stiff.

E. Correct.

Usage Tip

ℹ️ When *used to* appears in a question the best way of being correct and at the same time sounding natural is to make a simple statement and put the question at the end of the sentence – as in Sentence **E**.

v v v v **V** V V v v v

Vaccination: the cure that comes from cows

In a rhyme from yesteryear a man asks a milkmaid: 'What is your fortune, my pretty maid?' and is given the answer: 'My face is my fortune, Sir.' That confident reply is based on a medical breakthrough made by the English physician Edward Jenner, at a time when smallpox was both dreaded and widespread. It either killed its victims or left them scarred for the rest of their lives. Jenner's interest in the disease was quickened by a countryside tradition that smallpox did not affect milkmaids or anybody else who worked with cows and had caught the far less virulent disease of cowpox. In 1796 he cured an eight-year-old smallpox victim, James Phipps, by injecting him with cowpox. Since Latin was the language of science in those days and *vacca* is the Latin for cow, Jenner's method became known as vaccination.

vegetarian/vegan

A *vegan* goes one step further than a *vegetarian*. While *vegetarians* will not knowingly eat meat or fish, *vegans* avoid animal products entirely. Their diet cuts out milk, eggs, cheese and any other food that is derived from animals.

venal/venial/venery

These three words look alike and come fairly close to sounding alike, but have completely different meanings. *Venal* means 'open to bribery' and would be applied, for instance, in the case of a town hall official who, in return for cash or favours, moved applicants higher on a housing list. *Venial* means 'slight, pardonable or forgivable'. A Roman Catholic who commits a *venial sin* is not risking eternal damnation. *Venery*, a word that has fallen out of use, had two meanings. One was the pursuit of hunting and the other, which bequeathed to the language the word *venereal*, was the pursuit of sexual pleasure.

veteran/veterinary/veterinarian

The North American style of referring to ex-servicemen and women as *veterans* is now widely accepted in Britain and has largely replaced the term *old soldiers*. British usage, however, still prefers *veterinary surgeon* (often shortened to *vet*) to the American *veterinarian*.

veteran car/vintage car/etc

When the term *veteran car* was first used it applied only to cars made before 1905, but the qualifying date has shifted forwards with the passing years. It has now reached 1919 and is unlikely to move any further. The Vintage Cars Club recognises the following classifications:

Veteran – cars constructed up to 31 December, 1904. Only veteran cars may take part in the annual London to Brighton run. This celebrates the Emancipation Run which took place in 1896 upon the repeal of the so-called Red Flag Act. Before repeal there was a speed limit of 5 mph on public roads and cars could be driven only if they had man walking in front, carrying a red flag.

Edwardian – cars built from 1905 until the end of the First World War in 1918.

Vintage – cars made between the end of the First World War and the end of 1930.

Post Vintage Thoroughbred – cars dating from 1931 to the end of 1940, provided they meet certain quality standards, as do for instance Rolls Royce, Sunbeam, Lagonda, Alvis and Talbot.

Classic – this term is usually applied to quality cars built after 1945, the year that saw the end of the Second World War.

viable

This adjective, meaning 'capable of life' began as a medical term to describe a newborn child or a foetus that was likely to reach the stage of being born. It was extended to other forms of life, such as eggs, seeds and spores, that appeared to have the capacity for further development. In a further extension it came to be applied to any project that seemed destined for success – a business plan for instance. So far, so good, but *viable* has now become a vogue word that is used far too freely. If only to ring the changes, careful speakers will consider such alternatives as *possible, workable, feasible, likely, achievable* and *promising.*

W

waistcoat

The accepted pronunciation follows the spelling, but sticklers for tradition insist on *wess*-kit, or even go back to the days of Mr Pickwick's Sam Weller and say *vess-kit*.

wash up

If an American asks 'Would you like to wash up?' don't reach for a dishcloth and a tea towel. You are not being invited to do the dishes but simply to splash some water on your hands and face and have what we would call a wash and brush-up.

wave/waive

To make the right choice between these two, just call to mind this rather cynical statement: *Britannia may have ruled the waves but she also knew when to waive the rules*. Supposing your neighbour plans to build an extension that might reduce the value of your house, you can *waive* your right to object or you can *wave aside* the arguments put forward in support of the proposal.

we/us

The longer the sentence, the more room there seems to be for confusion to arise between these two.

TEST YOURSELF

A. It remains to be seen whether the new proposals will do much for we/us taxpayers in the middle income ranges.

B. Some people think it is at best irresponsible for we/us non-combatants to criticise some of the weapons used in modern warfare.

C. We/us local shopkeepers strongly object to the proposal to build a supermarket practically on our doorsteps.

ANSWERS
A. *Us*   **B.** *Us*   **C.** *We*

Usage Tip

ℹ️ Grammatically, the pronoun *we* is always the subject in a clause or sentence, performing an action, and *us* is the object on or for whom the action is performed. If there is any doubt about which to use, pare down the sentence so that only one of the competing pronouns is left and the right choice will immediately become clear. In Sentences **A** and **B**, for instance, you would not say *do much for we* or *irresponsible for we*. Nor, in Sentence **C**, would you say *Us shopkeepers object*.

CURIO CORNER

Weasel words

The sinuous, slender-bodied weasel has a reputation for being able to suck nourishment out of an egg, leaving only the shell. In much the same way, weasel words can suck the force and true meaning out of a message – especially an unwelcome one. In fairness it has to be admitted that weasel words may be used to avoid embarrassing the person on the receiving end. More often, however, it is the user who would be embarrassed by plain speaking.

What they say	What they very likely mean
We'll have to let you go	*You're fired*
Down-sizing	*A lot of people will be fired*
Right-sizing	*Ditto*
I want to spend more time with my family	*The Prime Minister thinks I'm not up to the job*

I hear what you say	*But I'm not going to do much about it*
I accept full responsibility for the mistake	*But if anybody pays with their job it won't be me*
That's a good question – I'm glad you asked it	*It's an awkward and embarrassing question, so give me time to think up an answer that will at least sound convincing*
Lessons will be learned	*But promptly forgotten once the heat dies down*
I'm passionate about climate change/chess/tiddlywinks (Pick almost any subject)	*I'm jumping aboard a bandwagon*
Let's move forward. I just want to get on with the job	*I have no defence to offer, so please drop the subject*
We take complaints like yours very seriously and your call is important to us, but all our lines are busy, so please wait	*But in reality there's not much much we can do about it. Calls are not so important that we are prepared to hire enough staff to answer them promptly*
Will you bear with me for a couple of minutes?	*I'm out of my depth and I need to find somebody who knows the answer, so be prepared for a long wait*
This call may be recorded and used for training purposes	*Don't shout, swear or abuse the staff – it will all be on record*
We are conducting a survey in your area	*We are going to try to sell you something*
It isn't you – it's me	*It isn't me – it's you*

A chain is only as strong as its weakest link	*You are the weakest link. Goodbye*
More in sorrow than in anger	*I'm loving this. You have annoyed me for long enough*
Customer (on a train)	*Passenger*
Edgy, on the edge (said of humour)	*Smutty, foul-mouthed, offensive*
A safe pair of hands	*Not likely to set the world on fire*
Stakeholder	*Taxpayer*
Team player	*Lacks initiative; can't work unsupervised*
Quantitative easing	*Pumping funds into a nation's banking system – in effect, printing money*
Redacted	*A cover-up, with names and/or other important information blanked out, often to protect the guilty*

well

Careful speakers deplore the way this once-modest adverb appears to be attaching itself, with the enthusiasm of a buttonholing bore, to just about any word that takes its fancy. Terms such as *well pleased, well tempered, well inclined, well heeled, well spoken* and *well dressed* have long been accepted as standard English, but such usages as *well delighted, well good, well angry, well interested* and *well hungry* are regarded as being at best slang and at worst trendily sloppy. The indiscriminate use of *well* as an intensifier, though it does not fly in the face of logic, is an offence against tradition. And there are, after all, many alternatives: *very, highly, fully, utterly, entirely, totally, completely, decidedly, markedly* or even, at the risk of sounding pompous, *to a considerable extent.*

were/was *See* subjunctive mood

whence

Unless you are deliberately attempting to sound jocular, think twice before dropping this word into your speech or writing. Above all, be wary of saying *from whence,* for *whence* already means 'from where'. Admittedly, the phrase has an impressive pedigree. Psalm 121 in the King James Bible reads: *'I will lift up mine eyes unto the hills, from whence cometh my help'*. But for better or for worse the language has moved on since King James was on the throne.

which/that

Fasten your seat belts. Even Henry Fowler, that towering figure among lexicographers, described the rules governing the choice between *which* and *that* as 'an odd jumble'. And that was around a century ago, when authorities on English usage knew how to be magisterially authoritarian. Fowler recognised that the rules on *which* and *that* could sometimes be ignored, and thought it sometimes excusable that many writers used *that* as if it were no more than an ornamental variation for *who* and *which*.

TEST YOURSELF
A. When are you planning to return the lawnmower which/that I lent you last summer?
B. May I remind you about my lawnmower, which/that cost me more than £300, and has been lying unused in your garage ever since you borrowed it.
C. I'm not inclined to lend you my gardening tools ever again, and nothing which/that you say will make me change my mind.
D. The back stairs, which/that were hardly ever used, led to a door which/that had not been opened for 30 years or more.

E. The mad dog tried to bite Henry, but it was the dog which/that died.

F. The birthday present which/that pleased Johnny most of all was a Swiss Army knife, which/that had been given to him by his grandmother.

G. You'll find the wine which/that you enjoyed so much last time on the top row of the rack.

H. This wine, which/that I bought in the local supermarket, is just right for sipping in the garden on a lazy summer afternoon.

I. My new computer is the most user-friendly of all the electronic devices which/that I have ever used.

J. John searched with mounting frustration for the wallet which/that he knew was somewhere in the house.

K. *The Catcher in the Rye* is one of the most entertaining books about being a teenager which/that was ever written.

ANSWERS

A. *That.*

B. *Which.*

C. *That* – or sidestep the problem by using neither word and choosing simply *nothing you say.*

D. *Which* for the seldom-used back stairs and *that* for the locked door.

E. *That.*

F. *That* for the pleasing present and *which* for the Swiss Army knife.

G. *That* – or say simply *The wine you enjoyed so much* …

H. *Which.*

I. *That* – or say simply *of all the electronic devices I have ever used.*

J. *Which.*

K. *That.*

Usage Tips

[i] If you are not already familiar with them, it helps to get to grips with some grammatical terms. When *which* and *that* are used to indicate a relationship within a sentence they are termed *relative pronouns*. There are two kinds of relative pronoun: *restrictive* and *non-restrictive*.

[i] *That* introduces a restrictive clause – one that defines the parent noun, differentiating it from all others of its kind, as in: *The cement that was delivered on Thursday has been out in the rain all night.*

[i] *Which* is non-restrictive and introduces a clause that simply describes the parent noun, or gives information that does not amount to a definition. Example: *The cement, which ought to have been stored more carefully, was delivered on Thursday.*

[i] If the clause is enclosed within commas or set between a comma and a full stop, this is a clear indication that it is non-restrictive, and the pronoun to use is *which*. Example: *The charm of Bath, which has an appeal for so many visitors, goes back to the days of Beau Brummel.*

[i] The restrictive pronoun *that* can sometimes be omitted without harming the sense of a sentence. Example: *Bath still has much of the charm (that) it had in Beau Brummel's day.* The non-restrictive pronoun *which* cannot be omitted in this way.

[i] *That* is normally used, rather than *which*, after *it is, it was, any, anything, everything, some, something, none* and *nothing* (see Sentences **C** and **E**). It is also used when the sentence refers to something that is outstanding or the best of its kind (see Sentences **I** and **K**).

[i] A rule of thumb that will help you in many instances to make the right choice is: *that* defines and *which* describes. So it's *The watch that you gave me last Christmas* but *The watch, which tells the date as well as the time, is self-winding.*

while

There are one or two pitfalls for the unwary.

TEST YOURSELF
A. John perched on the ladder, reaching out for apples, while Mary, below him on the ground, collected them in boxes.
B. While freedom of speech is highly desirable, nobody has the right to shout 'Fire!' in a crowded theatre – unless, of course, there is one.

C. The band on the *Titanic* played *Nearer, my God, to Thee* while the icy waters of the North Atlantic were rising towards their ankles.

D. Every soldier in the platoon turned to the sergeant, expecting him to get them out of a tight spot. While nobody thought of asking the lieutenant for his opinion.

E. While I disagree with just about every word you say, I cannot question your right to speak your mind as forcefully as you please.

F. Michael liked to relax by playing golf, while his sister tackled the crossword in *The Times*.

ANSWERS

A. Correct.

B. Correct.

C. Correct.

D. Incorrect.

E. Correct.

F. Incorrect; the sentence is ambiguous.

Usage Tips

[i] When *while* is used to indicate that two or more things are happening at the same time or that there is some other kind of equivalence between them, both or all should be mentioned in the same sentence. It is not acceptable to distribute time-linked events between separate sentences – as happens in Sentence **D**. But errors of this nature are by no means unusual. A comma after *spot* and a lower case *w* for *while* would correct the error in Sentence **D**.

[i] *While* can also mean *whereas* or *although*. This can sometimes lead to ambiguity, as in Sentence **F**. If Michael's sister is talented enough to tackle *The Times* crossword it is unlikely that she would take as long to solve it as Michael does to complete a round of golf. *Whereas* would be a better choice here than *while*. In Sentence **B** there is no ambiguity, but *although* would be just as good a choice as *while*.

whilst

In British usage, *whilst* is acceptable as an occasional variant for *while*, but it is beginning to sound whimsical and old-fashioned.

whisky/whiskey

If it's Scotch it's *whisky*. If it's Irish or American it's *whiskey*.

who/whom

The rules are clear: *who* refers to the subject of a sentence and *whom* refers to the object. In practice, choosing between them is not always simple. *Whom* can sound stiff and over-formal, and is increasingly being shouldered aside by *who* – especially when asking a question. This may dismay purists, but there are times when strict adherence to the rules is less important than relying on an idiom and sounding natural.

TEST YOURSELF
A. I don't care who/whom is chosen as captain so long as we get a top-class goalkeeper.
B. Who/whom were you with last night?
C. To whoever/whom it may concern: I will no longer be responsible for my wife's debts.
D. After John was turned down for promotion he complained: 'It's not what you know, it's who/whom you know.'
E. Who/whom do you think I bumped into at the supermarket the other day?
F. Whoever/whomever the police suspect, I will never believe that Sheila is the mastermind of a shoplifting gang.
G. Who/whom are you going to vote for in the next general election?
H. The jockey who/whom Jessica backed seems incapable of getting the best out of his horse.
I. '...never send to know for who/whom the bell tolls' (John Donne).
J. Do you think there is a special type of reader for who/whom this book is written?

ANSWERS

A. *Who.*

B. *Who* is acceptable because it is idiomatic. The grammatically correct *whom* sounds stilted.

C. *Whom.*

D. *Who.* Again, the grammatically correct *whom* sounds stiff and over-formal.

E. *Who,* because the grammatically correct w*hom* is far too formal for everyday speech.

F. *Whomever* is grammatically correct, but *whoever* is acceptable, even preferable, in an informal context.

G. *Whom* is correct but the idiomatic and more natural-sounding *who* is preferable.

H. *Whom.* If this sounds a shade too formal, use *that* or sidestep the dilemma by dropping the word and simply saying *The jockey Jessica backed.*

I. *Whom.*

J. *Whom.*

Usage Tips

[i] A quick way to settle which is the grammatically correct choice between *who* or *whom* is to answer the question that is asked or implied. In Sentence **B**, the answer could be either *him* or *her.* Grammatically, both of these are the objects of a verb, and call for *whom*, but idiom, which is stronger than logic, calls in this case for *who. He* and *she*, being subjects of the verb in any sentence, always call for *who.*

[i] There are many occasions when you will have to decide between being correct and sounding natural. Except in the most formal contexts it may be preferable to use the 'incorrect' version – as in Sentences **B, D, E** and **G**.

[i] That said, although it may sound slightly stiff, *whom* is almost always the word to use when, as in Sentence **J**, it comes directly after a preposition (*to, for, with, by* and so on).

why *See* **reason**

-wise

Adding *-wise* to a word – as in *Cashwise we have a problem,* or *Weatherwise, the outlook is unfavourable* – is an Americanism that has taken firm root in Britain although it has its detractors among traditionalists. They would prefer *We are running short of cash* or *The weather forecast is unfavourable.* Like many linguistic devices, *-wise* can be overused. But used intelligently it can also add a cheerful, defiant cockiness to many a statement. Never has it been employed more effectively than in the film *The Apartment,* in which the character played by Jack Lemmon tells a defeated rival who was over-fond of using the construction: *'That's how it crumbles, cookie-wise.'*

wisteria/wistaria

The climbing plant that brings a misty touch of lilac-blue to many a house front is named in honour of the American physician Caspar Wistar, but is spelled with an e: *wisteria.* The spelling *wistaria* is used for the genus, but not for the species.

women/girls/ladies/guys

Navigating between these words can lead into treacherous waters. Feminists, and especially those in the United States, prefer to be addressed as *women.* They see the term *girls* as being condescending. It is still generally acceptable, however, to refer to a *girlfriend,* in much the same way as a male might be called somebody's *boyfriend.* A neutral expression that could apply to either a woman or a man is *partner.*

However correct it may be most of the time, there are times when *women or woman* can sound disrespectful or even offensive – as, for example, when President Clinton claimed: 'I did not have sexual relations with that woman.'

Whether the term *lady* is accepted with a gracious smile or regarded as an affront depends on tradition as well as on intention. The title *Lady* for the daughter of a duke or the wife or widow of a knight or baronet is one that carries prestige. And it is a sign of respect to say that 'She always acts like a perfect lady'. But respect is not to the fore if, for example, somebody shouts: 'Hey, lady! Did you just drop that cat into a wheelie bin?'

The terms used in sport seem to owe more to tradition than to a desire to be consistent. The Olympic Games has its Women's Finals, as do the American tennis championships, played at Flushing Meadows. Wimbledon, however, holds on firmly to its Ladies Finals, and oarswomen at Henley compete for the Ladies Challenge Plate. Golf offers something for everybody. Among its governing bodies are both a Ladies' Golf Union and a English Women's Golf Association.

A recent innovation in the glitzy world of showbiz which has yet to make much of an impression outside that world is to address groups of mixed gender or even one composed entirely of women as 'You guys'.

Usage Tip

[i] With the signposts pointing in so many different directions it is not always easy to make the correct choice between *women, girls* and *ladies*. There are, however, two guidelines to follow. First, be sensitive to your audience. If there are feminists among them, address them as *women,* and above all avoid such terms as *girls* or *gals*. Secondly, if there is a tradition, follow it. If you are proposing a toast, make it to *ladies and gentlemen*. If your reference is to a sport, particularly one that is long established, *ladies* carries an aura of respect, but in some sports (see above) *women* is preferred. See also **sexist language**.

worth while/worthwhile

Purists maintain that there are two ways to set out this word. They would say: *Spending five or six years learning Latin is worth while,* but *Spending five or six years learning Latin is a worthwhile thing to do*. Most others have long abandoned the attempt to make a distinction and always write *worthwhile* as one word. Which side you take depends on how much importance you attach to tradition.

would *See* should

write

One of the few Americanisms that have made no inroads on Britain's side of the Atlantic is that instead of saying: 'I will write a letter to my brother tomorrow,' the American style is 'I will write my brother tomorrow'. In the British version *a letter* is the direct object of the verb *will write* and *my brother* is the indirect object. Using the indirect object as if it were a direct object is what makes the American version sound strange to British ears. What is going to be written is a letter, not a brother.

Xmas

Contracting Christmas to *Xmas* can offend many people – whether or not they are practising Christians. This is in spite of the fact that the abbreviation has a venerable history. The X is derived from the shape in the Greek alphabet of the first letter in the name *Kristos* (Christ). Anglo-Saxon monks, writing their manuscripts on parchment or vellum, used *Xmas* with not the slightest suggestion of irreverence. Nevertheless, *Xmas* is associated today with the commercialisation of Christmas. Those who use it give the impression that they are in too much of a hurry to write out the full word.

you know what I mean

This verbal tic, usually clamped on to a statement so banal that its meaning is obvious, can be both unnecessary and tiresome.

yours/your's *See* apostrophe

yourself *See* myself

yours faithfully/sincerely

The conventional way to close a business letter is with *Yours faithfully* the first time you write and *Yours sincerely* in letters that follow. When writing to a friend there are no conventions that must be followed. *As always … As ever… Kind regards … Best wishes … All the best … Bye for now… More Later… Love and Kisses … TTFN* (for those whose memories stretch back as far as Tommy Handley and ITMA) … whatever seems right.

zenith

In astronomy, a *zenith* is a high point in the remoteness of space, directly above the observer. The word has come to be applied to highest points in general – the *zenith* of a career, for example. If there is any possibility that a listener or reader may not be familiar with the word, consider using one of its synonyms. They include *peak, summit, supreme, utmost, acme,* and *maximum*. The antonym of *zenith* is *nadir,* the lowest possible point.

zucchini

This is the American and Italian name for what British and French cooks call courgettes.

SOME OTHER TITLES FROM HOW TO BOOKS

A GUIDE TO MODERN GAMEKEEPING
Essential information for part-time and professional gamekeepers
J C JEREMY HOBSON

This book is a comprehensive gamekeeping manual for those enthusiastic amateurs who spend their spare time running a small DIY syndicate shoot, and for those who are professionally employed on a full time basis. It shows the reader how to perform all the tasks required of the modern gamekeeper, including how to rear and release game and it advises on many aspects of habitat improvement and conservation. It also covers important and sometimes controversial issues, such as public access on private land, the need for predator and pest control, and many other aspects which need to be considered by keepers, be they part-time or professional.

ISBN 978-1-84528-497-8

HOW TO GET TO THE NORTH POLE
...and other iconic adventures
TIM MOSS
With a foreword by Ranulph Fiennes

This book will tell you how to row an ocean; get to the North Pole; cross a desert; sail the seven seas; cycle around the world; get to the South Pole; and climb an unclimbed mountain. Written by seasoned adventurer Tim Moss, it takes you through the details of each challenge or journey. If you're rowing an ocean where do you sleep at night? If you're at one of the Poles how do you go to the loo in temperatures way below sub-zero? If you're cycling round the world precisely what difficulties will you face and how will you overcome them? From armchair adventurer to those simply looking for practical advice, this book is aimed at anyone who's ever dreamed of doing something BIG!

ISBN 978-1-84528-490-9